*"This book tells all: the st*

*of comparison, of fear. It tells of the brokenness and the battle. But it also tells of the beauty. Gelly helps us dig up the good news that's in the battle: we are fully loved and fully free. We can breathe big, full breaths and own our big, full beauty and live big, full lives."*

**-Amy Seiffert, author of Chin Up: Wearing Grace Strength and Dignity When Motherhood Unravels Our Souls**

*"Gelly is a big ol' gulp of fresh air, breathing life into hopeless and joyless situations with her deep wisdom and authentic, hilarious vulnerability. She is a safe place to rest, to lay your walls down and let your truest self free. She's a cheerleader, and her resounding encouragement sings louder than the lies, because she's been there before and she's not afraid of who knows. Gelly, keep going. Breathe deeply, rest softly, and, girl, sing loudly."*

**-Colleen Eschweiler, Writer, Choreographer, Comedian**

*"What I love most about this book is that the walking-on-the-ledge-of-the-cliff vulnerability is much more than a pretty lesson tied up with a neat little bow; it is a lifestyle. Gelly writes with openness that would make most of us stop in our tracks, and she calls us into it with her. She fights for the freedom of our hearts in this book, but it's only so impactful because she lives it so well. Get ready for your courage to grow wings."*

**- Max, Trauma Counselor, Professor, Freedom Advocate**

*"Girlish Vigor is the kind of book that can change your world. Gelly not only writes and speaks freedom-soaked truth, she LIVES it. She doesn't just preach the importance of sharing the stage, it will be her legacy. She reminds everyone around her that the world suffers when we don't follow our dreams. She reminds us that God created us with*

*passions and gifts, whether they be homeschooling or Corporate America, entrepreneurship or foster care. He created us with gold inside and Gelly will not rest until everyone she knows and loves has fought to find it and live their best life. She is a trailblazer and a cheerleader. She earned her spot on stage through real struggles and dark seasons that forced her to dig deep, keep her eyes on Jesus, and fight for better. Her willingness to share how she continues to step into strength and out of silence is a gift to us all."*

**-Libby Romanin, Writer, Mama, Fierce Cheerleader**

*"It's rare for someone as gorgeous as Gelly to be the girl next door. And yet Gelly is. In her book "Girlish Vigor" she lets you into her heart, and you can't help but welcome her into yours as well. With courage, candor, compassion, and a touch of comedy, she shares what it means to really fall in love with yourself. She invites you to discover the dreams the Divine has for you in this book that's as open as her soul."*

**-Martha Chandran-Dickerson, Writer, Editor, Educator, World Traveller**

*"Gelly May is the most genuine and encouraging person I've ever known. When she says she wants to see the women around her shine, it's no joke. The best part about Gelly is that when she tells you to chase your dreams it's because she has been in the game, overcoming fear and chasing after her own dreams. I promise that you will come away from her book inspired and feeling like you just gained a new friend."*

**-Cassy Vollmar, Designer, Writer, Entrepreneur**

*"The clearest depiction I can give you for the esteem I have for Gelly is this: When the stress of motherhood takes over my time for self care, and I'm staring at my postpartum body in the mirror with tears streaming down my face, Gelly's the first person I'd call. Girlish Vigor is a resource to offer that same guidance to everyone who is fortunate enough to turn its pages. Gelly is wise beyond her years: She opens her mouth and changes the world."*

**-Leslie Hartley, Artist, Podcast Host, Mama**

*"Gelly is the friend who every woman wants in her corner. She will fight for you with passion—not because she has to but because she wants to. Speaking truth, love and encouragement through a framework of vulnerability is her gift. And that's what you're getting in Girlish Vigor—a gift. One that you can open page by page. So start unwrapping these words. Because as you do, you'll stand taller, hold your head higher, and rise up with girlish vigor. I can't think of any better gift than that!"*

**- Kati Thompson, Owner of Eden Fashion Boutique, Dreamer, Teacher, Lover of Community over Competition**

# GIRLISH ~~FIGURE~~ VIGOR

GELLY MAY

Stripping Off What Shrinks
and Stepping into Strength

Girlish Vigor


ISBN: 9781093999990



First printing April 2019 / Printed in the United States of America

*For Melódia Luz: you're the song that got me singing again, the story that got me writing again.*

*For my sisters: you never let me stay small or safe or tucked away behind my fears.*

*For my husband: who fought for me when I couldn't fight for myself, and who started it all: the originator of Girlish Vigor.*

# Introduction

I wish you could have seen me all those mornings squeezing my Cuban thighs into a pair of skinny, skiiiiinnnnnyyy, jeans.

It took:

- One olympic-style vertical leap in the air
- Two deep squats
- Two and a half violent hip thrusts
- And finally, a few lunges across the bedroom to seal the deal.

But I got them on. That's right; starting the day with a victory. They were on and we were *one*. We were *soaring*. We were...counting the minutes until we could take them off.

A pair of too-tight pants at the bottom of my closet that I reserved for "someday"? Oh, I eyed those bad boys like I was a gladiator and they were the denim dragon I must slay. *You WILL fit me or I will DESTROY you.* I don't care how much of my upper butt pops over the top of the waistband.

You feel me, right ladies?

You and I have gotten reeeeaaally good at squeezing into things, haven't we? Sucking in, squishing, smooshing, getting small, all so we can fit into what we think we should *wear* or who we think we should *be*. We have a system for it—a dance, if you will. Trends bend and we try our darndest to touch our toes right alongside them. Our weight fluctuates and so does the elasticity of our Spanx. Our schedules spread thin and we still find a way to squeeze just *one* more thing in.

I even tried to squeeze *this book* into what I thought it was supposed to be, which is why it took 17.5 titles and two *full years* of writing before it became what it was supposed to be.

It started out as a guide for "holistic healing from depression," with plans, steps, science, stats, research...basically all of the things you *don't* want to hear about when you're actually depressed. And halfway through the book, I ran into a serious problem.

I was depressed. Again.

*Crap*. That wasn't part of my super-put-together-professional-author plan.

I had gone six years without a real "relapse," and yet there I was, lifeless and tired and teary for too many days in a row. And who wants to read a guide to get out of depression by a girl who was barely doing it herself?

No one.

When I finally stopped trying to squeeze words into a mold and just let them flow freely, pieces of me that I hadn't heard for a while started whispering again, and the freedom that gave me, to my surprise, actually started to lift the depression fog.

When I felt it lifting, that's when it hit me: my story, my shutting down, my staying small and sad, even my diagnosed *illness* wasn't *just* about a predisposition to a chemical imbalance. Or about trauma rewiring my brain. *Or* about needing the right essential oils, anti-inflammatory nutrition, or exercise plan. All of these mattered but they weren't the root of the matter.

The real problem, the true root issue, was this: I had learned only *one* way to survive my entire life.

No matter what was thrown at me, or to those around me, I had *one* default response: shut down. Shrink. Stay small. Scared. Sad. But more than anything else, safe, because "safe" is where things hurt less.

Safety: it was low to the ground, out of the way. I hid and unpacked there and assumed it was my only vantage point because I'm not worthy of a greater view (that's for the other girl, the one that has it all together, the one with married parents, a clean, uncomplicated past, body weight that stays off easily, and cheeks that don't redden when her heart pounds. That vantage point was *not* for me). And so the woman I wanted to be—who I was created to be—was slowly disappearing until I completely lost her.

And I did.

I lost her.

For 27 years.

But who's counting.

In its most basic definition, "depression" is the action of *lowering something or pressing something down,* and since all I knew was life on the ground, it was easier to just write that diagnosis across my forehead and stay there. Depression may have been the soundtrack that set the tone for the musical that was my life, but it wasn't the villain. It wasn't the thing shrinking me. This is not to say that I wasn't depressed or that I didn't experience seasons where I needed major intervention, but the diagnosis wasn't the end of the story, it was just the beginning.

This book, you guys. It dug up the human I was created to be, the one that's been hiding, and told it, "Show your face, woman. The *real* one." And it was good to see that face, even if I hardly recognized her at first glance (picture Tom Hanks in "Castaway" the first time he sees himself after being stranded alone on an island for years.) She was deflated, hungry, hardly breathing. Hardly living. Her lungs were collapsing, so to speak, because what rib cage can bear that much pressure for that long? And she was talking to a volleyball with a smiley-face drawn on it. Only it wasn't a volleyball. It was my 3-month-old daughter smiling up at me in between diaper blowouts. I smiled back through tears even though it took every ounce of strength I had left.

Why was it so hard for me to speak freely without second guessing everything that came out of my mouth? Why couldn't I sing (or share my voice at all) without my throat closing and my eyes crying? Why did I shut down so easily around some people? Why was I always on the edge of crippling depression? Why was I so prone to panic attacks? And WHY, for pete's sake, WHY couldn't I remember what it felt like to *just be me*, freely?

Well, it's really hard to do anything freely when you're not breathing freely, whether it's your soul or your body that's being suffocated. I had no idea I had grown accustomed to functioning with less air. You know, like when you're wearing a tight dress? That one that almost wouldn't quite zip all the way up? You never realize you haven't been taking full breaths all evening until you take the dress off at the end of the night and your rib cage can fully expand again. Fun fact: 300 years ago, the first corset was invented. It was the first time that we as women were physically given an actual mold to squeeze into. But we've been trying to squeeze into things and living small, safe lives *way* longer than that.

So. I've been stripping off everything that I spent 27

years trying to squish myself into, and this book is my big, full, beautiful breath—a breath much overdue after a long night of restricted breathing.

These are all the things I had to (and am continuing to) strip off of my life, my heart, and my body in order to *breathe*, live *freely*, and be my most authentic best self.

Here's the scoop: I wrote down all the stories I could possibly think of where I knew I had been living small. These stories represent the corset: all the things squeezing the life out of me. I counted six greater themes as the stories unraveled, six strings I needed to cut off of the corset in order to be freed, and then I put the stories somewhere within those six strings.

On top of the stories, since I *love* me some brave fashion (and since in most places around the world streaking is frowned upon), we're stripping *off* what shrinks us down and stepping *into* a new outfit; one we feel absolutely *incredible* in. For each of the six strings we loosen, we also have a #GVOOTD—a "Girlish Vigor outfit of the day"—both metaphorically speaking and for real. You'll see what I mean. Get excited! It's gonna be terrifying and awesome and freeing and great.

There are some stories that I hope make you pee your pants laughing and others that I couldn't write without crying, but all the stories have one purpose in mind:

fighting the smallness narrative I found myself living in and finding freedom from those things (or people) that were keeping me small, sad, and safe, so that I could live in *strength* and *freedom*. I found a way to cross out everything I thought I was supposed to be, like *a cute and small and not-too-curvy girlish figure*, and I'm replacing it with the truth: I was created to breathe, stand, and live in strength.

This is my Girlish ~~figure~~ Vigor.

Oh—and by the way:

*Breathing freely* is quite a contagious thing; you just might catch it.

I hope you're wearing your stretchy pants.

# CONTENTS

# THE DOUBLE-KNOT

## 1
# "I need to use the restroom:"

*Frequently used euphemism implying the need to relieve oneself. Most often used when the subject feels awkward saying, "I have to poop."*

No one says "I have to use the restroom" when they just have to pee. It's pretty normal in most contexts to casually say, "I'm just gonna go pee real quick!" But when we have to *go number two,* all of a sudden we become part of the royal family and announce that we must "*use the restroom.*"

So, since you and I just met and I don't know where you stand on conversations about bodily functions, I'm going to ease into this story with as much class as I can muster up:

I sat on the couch with *the cutest boy ever* while we watched a movie. I had to "*use the restroom*" so bad that my stomach was making those terrible upward-rumble, internal-flatulence noises (don't pretend you don't know what I'm talking about, Queen Elizabeth.) I remember sitting there in utter panic, dreading the next quiet scene of the movie because my stomach would rumble SO LOUDLY and that *cutest boy ever* kept asking, "Are you *sure* you're not hungry? Do you want something to eat?", and I, of course, was trying to be the *coolest girl ever*, so I insisted that while yes, those were simply hunger growls and *nothing else*, I strangely did not want a single bite to eat.

Poor *cute boy*.

He was either super confused by my rejecting his attempt to nourish me as I practically starved to death next to him, or he knew *exactly* what I was doing but felt too awkward to say anything. Little did I know that while that boy *was* indeed cute, there was a *handsomest man ever* I would meet about six years later that I would end up marrying, so I should have just said, "NO BRO, I'M NOT HUNGRY, I JUST HAVE TO POOP. It's cool if you no longer want to make out with me."

End Scene.

All right. If you're still here, now I *know* we can be friends.

I struggle to trust people who aren't willing to talk at least *semi-openly* about bodily functions. If you get eye-rolley from hearing me talk about something as human as "*using the restroom,*" I don't even want to know what you'll think when I tell you that one time I led my husband on a CAR CHASE through town during one of our biggest fights, or that I gave birth to my daughter (an almost-ten-pound-mammoth-of-a-baby) on my bedroom floor. But we'll get there.

In all fairness, this isn't actually about poop. The real takeaway of this story is that I have a serious issue with *quiet rooms.* Yeah, I know, most people have common dislikes and aversions to things like mushrooms, math equations, and Mondays. I, however, have an aversion to rooms that are too quiet. And no, not the kind of quiet where you get to breathe sitting alone in your living room; I *love* that kind of quiet. I'm talking about the kind of quiet that happens when we're with each other.

I can count *maybe* three or four good things that come from quiet rooms and they all start with the letter S—sleep, solitude, study, and...babymaking. But *most* quiet rooms, man, they give me the heebeegeebees.

They are the microphones that magnify our humanity yet make us want to hide it. For example, that time you laughed too hard during an inappropriate, quiet moment and got kicked in the leg by your mom to shush up and stay prim and proper? Or that time at church when your toddler would NOT stop wailing and you had to bounce up and down a hallway with her by yourself for an hour in order to not disturb everyone else? Or—the real kicker—that gas that you're holding in at the coffee shop *right now*? There is just no sure way to know if it's going to be as silent as you think it will, so you'd better hope that place is bumpin' with chatty customers to cover up the aftermath of the bean burrito you had for dinner last night.

Quiet rooms make us forget that everybody—*eeeverybody*—cries, laughs, poops, and toots. But we forget. It's almost like we have an internal Quiet Room Belief system that we all live by. It convinces us that, a) I am the only one experiencing or feeling this specific thing right now. (Which is always false, by the way. There is a 100% chance someone else is also feeling what you are and doing everything within their power to hide it as well.) and b) I am SO loud right now. Everyone is staring at me and is judging me. (Also false. Nobody cares, and if they do, they've got bigger issues.)

The thing is though, I've noticed sometimes I take the Quiet Room Belief System and apply it to my life even if the room is actually quite *loud*.

## 2
# Silent Night

My friend Amy hosts an annual Christmas party, and she has one of the most beautiful, pinterest-perfect homes you've ever seen in real life. When you arrive, you look into a living room fully decked out in soft string lights, flowing into a kitchen with a chic concrete countertop island chock-full of the biggest spread of expensive artisan cheeses you've ever seen, that continues flowing into a quaint little sunroom housing a perfectly asymmetrical hipster-Christmas tree, and outside the sliding french doors of the sunroom you spot a huge outdoor fireplace built next to an elegant outdoor bar (with even more chic concrete countertops) stocked with eggnog martinis that flow like a river and taste like liquid glory. Finally, you see people—lots and lots of people. Even with the large, open floor plan, it's often a standing room-only party.

It's a big deal in our town, too, because it's *fancy* (ahem...we're a cozy little t-shirts and yoga pants 24/7 kind of place), it only happens once a year, and getting an invite kind of feels like you've been invited to a New York City VIP holiday party. We get to wear cocktail dresses and load up on eyeliner. We also wake up the next day with ringing ears and hoarse throats because in order to hear yourself speak you have to essentially yell in someone's face all night.

But, even with all its dreamy once-a-year VIP goodness and all the fun noise and holiday cheer, most years it gets really quiet for me.

I tune out all the delightful laughter, music, and whisper-yelling, and *my pounding heart* is what I begin to hear loudest, along with all the overwhelming thoughts that come rushing in with it:

*Are my bangs falling in the right place?*

*Does that girl hate me?*

*Does that guy think I'm annoying?*

*I'm pretty sure no one here likes me.*

*Yep. Definitely. They all hate me.*

*Does my outfit look stupid?*

*I should've worn the pants. My knees definitely look fat.*

*Oh crap there's a lull in this conversation, better get a drink in my hand so I can take sips during the lulls and feel less awkward.*

*Oh thank God, there's the cheese table. More cheese. Less chat.*

*I have to pee. I should check my phone anyway. I am sure everything is falling apart at home and the babysitter needs me to come home. Dangit, the baby is being an angel. I'll just sit on this toilet and get on Instagram for a second and breathe in the bathroom.*

*What! How long has that thing been in my tooth? My friends are terrible. How could they not tell me? Oh right, probably because they hate me.*

And on, and on, and on the thoughts go.

Please tell me you've been here before. Not just stuck in the bathroom at a party, toilet-Instagramming to escape, but completely *stuck in your own head; a*ssuming no one *really* likes you, or, if they do, they are definitely torn about *how much* to like you because they are also judging you, your outfit choice, and your entire life.

I think that sometimes quiet rooms become our lifestyle as women. The noise of the room is stifled by the loudness in our minds as it echoes into every square inch of our bodies. It's the reason I thought I was introverted for almost 27 years: it wasn't that being around people drained me; it was my *mind* that drained me when people were around.

However.

This year, I decided to be brave at that VIP Christmas party.

I wore a brave outfit: heels, a corduroy mini(ish) skirt, a crop top, and big hair (and if you care to look, you can still find the picture on my Instagram where I talk about wearing brave things at that exact party under the hashtag #gvootd).

But most importantly, I dressed my *mind* up in brave things: I assumed that everyone else was just as anxious as I was. That they too went through four potential outfits and a quasi-temper tantrum trying to get ready. That they were standing around bravely hoping no one else would notice their nerves or call attention to their flaws. So I walked in with a soft, brave heart. I hugged everyone I saw. I told the women they looked flawless. I laughed *loudly*. I cut my usual verbal filter down by about half, choosing to speak freely and refusing to overthink every freaking thought that came into my mind. I cracked dumb jokes. I danced in the kitchen with my friend Libby even though we most likely looked like absolute loons (and the pastor of our church was definitely within view and definitely thought we were crazy. We danced anyway).

I didn't take my phone into the bathroom. I got out of my head and into the moment. I gave love freely because I assumed everyone was doubting, just as I was, whether or not they were wanted and loveable. I whisper-yelled and listen-yelled. I ate cheese. At one point, I literally announced to the 3-4 women standing around me that I wanted to "check out the outdoor fireplace" because I was having weird gas from all the cheese. It made the circle of women around me loosen up a little (maybe they had gas too? I'll never know!)

We feel so weighed down by other people's opinions of us or by what we *think* other people's opinions of us are. Not only do we feel weighed down, but sometimes, we are so completely crippled that we even decide not to try. We stay home, because those moments of awkwardness (by the cheese table when we take a bite of something we don't really want to eat, just because we don't know what to do with our hands) are too risky, too scary, too quiet.

How often do I assume I am the only one feeling the things I'm feeling? SO often, I've lost count.

How often do I assume everyone is judging me and has an opinion on my life? Even MORE often.

But this year's party was such a turning point for me. I've sloooowly been learning to quiet my mind and bathe in the sounds around me, rather than quieting the room and drowning in my thoughts. It's just awareness, really, that has started to free me up. Mindfulness is the first step for me when it comes to stripping off the opinions of other people—I have to pay attention to what I'm listening to.

I step into a moment, an event, a place and think to myself, *Am I bathing or drowning right now?*

For me, *bathing* is being present in the moment: I am sitting still and allowing myself to hear sounds as they come. I am sitting in it and feeling it flow around me like warm bath water, enveloping me. It feels quiet in my head as I observe the sights and hear the sounds. I am grounded, breathing, and choosing to step into it all.

*Drowning*, however, is when I can hardly hear what's happening around me because wave after wave, thoughts keep pummeling me. I feel foggy as I try to take in what's around me and it feels so loud in my head, and so unbearably quiet in the room. I can hardly take in what anyone says to me. I am drifting out of control, drowning, lost at sea.

The reason this was such a crucial realization for me was that so much of my anxiety was rooted in others' opinions of me. It made it really hard to go anywhere or do anything without feeling overwhelmed. If I'm constantly drowning before even dipping my toe into a moment, of course I'd rather stay on the shore where it's safe.

3

# On Opinions

I would be lying to myself if I said other people's opinions of me don't matter. Yes, I admit, the people-pleaser in me wants you to like me. And I don't have to feel guilty about that or embarrassed that I have yet to reach the "enlightenment" where I don't care about such *silly things*. But the thing is it's not silly at all. I am innately wired to care. I am wired to want to belong, to be loved, to be liked, and that is a *beautiful* thing, not a *shameful* one.

At the root of me caring about other people's opinions is the strong, beautiful, human desire to be loved. But I think we can simultaneously *want* to be liked by everyone, while accepting that not everyone *is* going to like us. We can have peace with that. And it's okay. It's okay because we have our trusted people, whose input *truly* matters, whose opinions are truly trusted.

However, I've noticed that if I'm not being proactive about what fills me up, I go desperately looking for "love" in all kinds of places. Places like, the opinions of people whose voices, quite frankly, haven't earned the right to hold weight in my life. I may *care* about everyone's opinion of me, but that doesn't mean I have to *listen* to everyone's opinion of me. So I've been learning to listen to opinions when love, and only love, is at the root. When love isn't at the root, *those* are the opinions I have to be willing to walk away from. Because remember, if the actual reason I care about people's opinions is that I desire to be loved, then opinions not in love are not for me.

# 4
# Panic

All throughout high school, I would sit at my desk during quiet moments in class and try to breathe really slowly from start to finish because of a tendency I had to start coughing uncontrollably *for no reason at all.* Sometimes the coughing spells would get so out of control that my eyes would start twitching involuntarily, which, let me tell you, is a *total* turn on for the hot guys sitting around you in class.

I would sit at my desk, sweating bullets, terrified I would feel that tickle start in at the back of my throat, or feel that heart-pounding sensation that meant a coughing attack was impending, AND terrified the teacher would ask me to read anything or answer any questions out loud.

No, I wasn't smoking in the boys room (although there was plenty of those sorts of shenanigans in my partying days, but we'll cover those juicy details later), and no, I wasn't suffering from whooping cough or asthma or anything like that. The coughing was actually psychosomatic, which is just a fancy way of saying that my brain knew the *only* way to get out of that classroom was to be excused to go to the bathroom. So, my panicked mind made me involuntarily cough until I was blue in the face and there was no other choice but for the teacher to say, "Why don't you go ahead and get a drink of water?" I promise I'm not making this up; remember, I thought boys were really hot, and non-stop coughing and twitchy eyes is *not* a way to win them over. I know it sounds crazy, but our bodies can get *really* creative in how they express stress.

It's hard to admit even now, but the *real* cause of my psychosomatic coughing-panic attacks—and what I was actually most terrified of—was sounding stupid. Classrooms were the very place when you needed to sound not-stupid in order to survive when the teacher would randomly call on you to read out loud. I was so afraid others would think I was just a dumb girl because it took me three times as long to read and understand something than it did the other kids. And on a deeper level, I was absolutely horrified that the truth was that I really *was* stupid. I'd walk into a classroom and the tapes in my head would start playing:

*I'm stupid.*

*Everyone thinks I'm stupid.*

*I'm not smart enough for this.*

*I'm too dumb to understand it.*

*I should just stop trying.*

*My brain doesn't work well.*

*I'm stupid.*

This internal feedback loop left me crushed. Paralyzed. Breathless (and I mean that quite literally, as I would gasp for air between coughing fits).

A wise counselor once told me that at the root of any panic attack is the fear of death. So, how did my feeling "stupid" actually stem from a fear of *death*? It was the death of a piece of me—a smart, talented, worthy, invaluable piece of me—that I kept repeatedly going to funerals for. It was my value, worth, and my voice that was dying. And those mini-funerals came in so many different shapes and sizes depending on the day.

My anxiety and panic launched my brain into fight or flight mode every time I walked into that classroom. I wasn't stupid at all, I was surviving.

Some days, both in and out of the classroom, my anxiety felt like a gorilla was using my chest as a trampoline. Other days, it felt like my head was a shaken up coke bottle: fizzy with overthinking, ready to explode, obsessing over every single freaking thing that could happen, every little thing that I said wrong or *might* say wrong.

It might feel totally different for you, but I don't know if I've ever met a woman who could honestly say she's never felt a moment of anxiety in her life. And for most of us, it's not just a single moment. It's perpetual, anxious existence. Shrinking, squeezing and overthinking is our default.

So maybe we can ask ourselves, is every single person in this room (or this world) a trusted soul whose opinion holds weight in our lives? Was everyone in that classroom someone whose opinion of us actually mattered because they loved us unconditionally?

No. The answer is most likely no.

But like many of us, I didn't see it at the time. I felt so insecure in who I was, whether or not I belonged, and if I was truly loved, that I held every single person's opinion closely to my heart. And I felt the weight that I was never quite enough or I was too much for them.

So much of my anxiety came from believing that who I was at my core needed to be somebody different than who I truly was in order to be loved by everyone. So I'd squeeze myself into being someone I'm not. I'd ignore the cry in my soul when I felt shut down by others, because, well, maybe they're right, anyway. Maybe the world is better off with this other version of me.

But what happens when we live a lifetime of squeezing and shrinking? Years later, my friend Brenda helped answer this question for me. She was a beautiful woman in her early sixties that exercised at one of the gyms I used to work for at the start of my career. She came in everyday, passing me by with a shy smile, never saying much. But I was so intrigued by her because she had more muscle than most people half her age. One day I finally drew up the courage to talk to her. I wanted to pick her brain; I was curious about her routines and relationship with exercise (I was impressed! She looked so good for her age...and any age really! I wanted to know her secret Mr. Miyagi wisdom!) But she had very little interest in talking about working out. Maybe she sensed my over-eagerness for a lean, tone, hourglass figure as a young woman in the early stages of her career in the fitness industry, because rather than discussing exercise, she put on her most loving, firm, mama bird tone and told me how little it all really mattered.

She said she worked out everyday now because she loved staying limber and feeling her body move, but not for a certain physique. In her young adulthood, corsets and waist training were a normal part of life, especially as a fitness model and competitor. She looked me square in the face and said that her body will actually never again function normally because of the damage those waist trainers caused. Can you imagine? Organs shifted and smooshed from years of shrinking. Her insides were all twisted up now, she explained, while gesturing with her hands to illustrate a knot in front of her stomach. I thought about how I *feel* like my insides are all twisted up on the days when I'm anxious, while hers *literally* were.

It's so hard for us to measure how our souls are shrinking or getting all twisted up, but this imagery of a corset helps me a lot. I felt so shocked when she was talking that I didn't do much besides listen. But afterwards, I asked Google what squeezing into a corset for years does to our bodies. Brenda was right, the health risks were a long, long list:

Rearranged internal organs.

Compromised fertility.

Damage.

Exhaustion.

Weakness.

Depletion.

Difficulty breathing.

Difficulty thinking clearly.

Even though I had never actually worn a *real* corset, it all sounded so familiar.

## 5
# Wired

As I kept reading the history and health risks of the corset, at one point I felt so overwhelmed that I just stopped dead in my tracks, grabbed a pen and wrote these words down in my journal.

*Dear heart,*

*You've been walking around wearing things that are too heavy and too small. You must be so tired. Please forgive me for shrinking to fit into molds that weren't made for you to begin with. I'm going to start stripping off everything that shrinks you down and start stepping into what makes you breathe fully. Even if it scares me.*

*Love,*

*Me*

Please tell me I'm not the only weirdo who writes notes to herself?

I get sad at the idea that I've been walking around not taking full breaths most of my life. It's overwhelming. I read more facts about corsets on Wikipedia like "Some women were laced so tightly that they could breathe only with the top part of their lungs. This caused the bottom part of their lungs to fill with mucus. Symptoms of this include a slight but persistent cough, heavy breathing."

And I just *know* some of the ways in which we get "laced tightly" throughout our lives are often impossible to see when they happen to us.

For nearly 350 years, a woman's primary means of support was the corset, with laces and stays made of whalebone or metal. In a way, it's been over 300 years of this "corset existence" both literally and figuratively. I know it sounds dramatic because most of us don't actually walk around wearing corsets that rearrange our insides, but how long have the things or people in your life that have been lacing you tightly gone unnoticed by you? How long have you been taking short, shallow breaths, or feeling weight on your chest and just assumed it was the way you are naturally wired? Five years? 50 years? Five minutes? Whatever the amount of time, it is *too long.*

300 years of brainwashing. We were born into it, and didn't stand a chance against the programming we've been handed generation after generation. Am I being too dramatic? Maybe a little, hehe—I tend to do that. But all melodrama aside, please take a second to really chew on this: if you google corsets and fashion in the 19th century, you'll see that a common term used was "silhouette". The silhouette of women's fashion literally means that whatever part of the woman's body the fashion industry was pushing to be a certain size was how they designed the corsets, so

that we could LITERALLY squeeze ourselves into societal expectations and fit the mold. Ugh. That means that we haven't *just* been subliminally manipulated all along, we have actually been overtly manipulated at times. There was a time when we wanted so desperately to fit the mold that that was what the fashion industry gave us: a real-life mold to squeeze into. Listen, sister: I can hardly stand a full day of wearing real pants. I cannot even imagine an entire lifetime of squeezing into a metal cage and calling it normal, let alone, beautiful.

I think this is a classic case of a good thing gone bad: our desire for belonging, love of beauty, and care for others—all beautiful things—out of balance, become weight we were never meant to carry.

# 6
# Empathy

Most of us ladies have empathy weaved into every fiber of our being; it's an incredibly beautiful gift we get to give the world. You want to know who is changing the world? It's the courageous, tender-hearted, compassionate woman who feels deeply when others suffer—so deeply that it springs her into action to lend a helping hand.

But sometimes, we take it a bit far. We try to carry everyone else's feelings, so that they don't have to. Empathy out of balance is taking responsibility for the emotions of other people instead of allowing them to feel it themselves. But fully feeling our emotions is part of being fully human. So when we try to stop someone from feeling, we're actually taking away part of their humanity. To rob someone of the experience of evolving in emotional intelligence is not loving, even if it *feels* loving in the moment. Empathy relates. Empathy sits. Empathy listens. Empathy says, "Me too", it doesn't say "Me instead."

We are empathetic, emotional, incredible beings. We feel deeply and are affected deeply by the feelings of others. But with the inherent value of a gem such as empathy there is an increased chance of robbery. Like any light, there is darkness at its edges—it's what makes the light so significant. With our gems of love, harmony and unity, there is an accompanied twistedness in most of us that we haven't figured out how to untangle for centuries.

We care more about the opinions of others than we do about truth.

We care more about the opinions of others than we do about love.

We care more about the opinions of others than we do about health.

We care more about the opinions of others than we do about almost anything.

And it's poisoning us. It poisoned our great-grandmothers, our grandmothers, our mothers, ourselves, and it's poisoning our daughters. If we don't put an end to it, who will?

# 7
# Breaking Free

Freedom trips me up sometimes. What I *want* it to mean most of the time is that I get to do whatever I want, when I want. You know, like sit in my car and eat a box of donuts by myself while listening to a podcast on nutrition. Of course I never did that exact thing in real life on a cool October afternoon, approximately around 3 PM while also wearing my softest jeans and black sweatshirt that showed all the powdered sugar evidence on it! I would *never* do such a thing. Neither would you, right? Riiiight?

If I base freedom—something every human should have—solely on what I "want", then I have to believe that I would not have lived past the age of two.

Do you know what my two-year-old daughter *wants* to do most days? She wants to eat batteries, use the top of our kitchen island like a trampoline, and stick crayons in her ears. One day she will thank me for how 'mean' I was for depriving her of the things she was certain she wanted most. I laugh at her insane impulses, but am I really all that different from her? I think at the core, I'm the same; I've just gotten better at pretending to be mature, or even convincing myself that what I want is actually what is best; I can convince myself of almost anything.

Have you ever wanted something SO bad, but then when it didn't happen and you looked back years later, you were SO grateful you didn't get what you wanted? Like that guy I cried SO MUCH over in high school: I was sure he was the man I wanted to be with forever, but now that I'm married to Ricky (who is the actual man of my dreams) I see how that high school guy couldn't stack up and I'm grateful I didn't get what I wanted at the time. Other times, it's been a job I was certain I needed, a house, an opportunity, an outcome. So many times I've looked back and been thankful that God's plan was better than what I wanted.

Since it's been a pattern I've observed in my life, I have *slooowly* (and I mean dying-90-year-old-turtle-slow) started proceeding with caution when I'm presented with something I want. Because of that, my definition of real freedom has *slowly* been shifting (again, we're talking ridiculously slow: the turtle is dead at this point and is decomposing into the earth to come back as a beautiful budding flower.)

I don't want the freedom to do whatever I want, I want the freedom to *be* whoever I want.

Those are two very different things. Because if I'm being honest, do I want to be the kind of woman who hides in her car and eats a box of donuts even though in some moments I am completely convinced that what I want most is a box of donuts? Nope. That kind of woman spends a lot of time having diarrhea the next day, breaking out in zits, and not being able to think clearly because gluten-sugar-brain-fog is no joke. The reality is that when I think I absolutely want or "need" the donuts (or the job/ alcohol/boyfriend/approval of others/etc.), that thing or person gains control over me, and then I'm right back in a corset that's suffocating me.

Listening to what I want to *do most*, rarely leads to real freedom. But listening to *who I want to be most* is where the real magic is.

The beautiful thing is that when I am focused with a clear vision of who I want to be, I am rarely bogged down or distracted by who I *don't* want to be. Pursuit is so much stronger than prevention—but they are so similar it's easy to conflate them.

*Prevention* is when I look at a box of donuts and think, "Is this really who I want to be?", chances are, I will convince myself one donut never killed anyone (which is true! Duh! Eat the donut, Gelly. Let's not get crazy here.)

*Pursuit* is when I look at the sticky note on my dashboard with three dreams about who I want to be as a woman, and then I don't even flinch as I drive by the donut shop because my eyes are stuck on that sticky note (and the road, because I am a responsible driver). I'm filled with hope and vision for my path—the box of donuts are nowhere on my radar.

This is my new approach to most things: I'm focusing on *pursuing* who I *want* to be instead of *preventing* who I *don't want to be*, and it's so freeing because I'm motivated by *joy* instead of by *guilt*.

Remember in driving school when the instructor told us not to look at the thing on the side of the road because wherever your eyes are, that's what the steering wheel turns toward? You'll end up in a ditch if you let yourself be distracted. It's the same concept. Set your eyes on who you want to be. You'll drive right by who you're avoiding without realizing. All of a sudden you'll be in a totally different *state* (both mentally, physically, and geographically—see what I did there?) If you want to get to Florida, think about Florida, look for Florida signs, follow a map to Florida, hear podcasts about Florida as you drive to Florida, and wear a bathing suit as you sit in the driver's seat because you are a free independent woman with both class *and* sass and are practicing being comfortable in your skin for your Saturdays on the beach. Don't hope to be a Floridian and then get so nervous you're going to get off on the wrong exit that you take your eyes off the Florida signs and end up taking the wrong exit anyway.

Real freedom is taking the time to figure out who you want to be. And then keeping your eyes on that woman—who she is, Who she believes in, what she's about.

So what does that look like in real life? Well, what I want is to please my mom and never ever disappoint her. What I want is to never rock the boat with my husband, my mother-in-law, or my friends, and instead always remain their favorite person that they never ever think low of. What I want is for that random person at the grocery store that I will never see again in my life, to think I am the most calm, put-together mom ever with peerless parenting techniques and a docile toddler to prove it. What I want is a box of donuts delivered to my door every time I start my period (and then another box when my period is over, because I need to celebrate, and then a box during the in-between week because that's the one week I'm not bloated and #yolo #treatyoself.) Oh, and I also want to wake up and have a six pack after eating those three boxes of donuts.

But *who* do I want to be?

I want to be a truth-teller, even if it means sometimes there's tension. I want to be a woman you can trust in every context because my actions have proven I value authenticity and honesty over people-pleasing or flattery. I want to be a driven dreamer, a fierce cheerleader, a leader.

I want to be in the midst of the most mundane moments and stand grateful and hunt for gems in myself and others. I want to *look* like a healthy person because I *am* a healthy person—not because I completed a quick-fix diet program, but because my entire lifestyle is balanced and healthy. I also want to be the kind of person that can rest well—specifically, on the beach, in Florida, in a two-piece that I love and feel like Beyoncé in, regardless of how many babies I've pushed out (because, let's be honest, the wedgies in a one piece are no joke and I'd rather show some loose skin and some jiggle than have Satan himself riding up my butt all day.)

# 8
# A Final Confession

You have to promise me you won't write me off as a crazy person when I tell you what I'm about to tell you. I'll give you a second, you decide if you're going to stick around.

...

Still there?

Great.

Listen, sometimes, we believe in Santa Claus, or we believe in unicorns, or we believe that a tiny fairy comes at night and takes the tooth that just fell out of our mouth and gives us not monopoly money but real money. We've all believed in things that have absolutely no real scientific proof or grounding and held them as our Holy Grails.

So, hopefully you can at least have some empathy for me. Here goes nothin'.

Sometimes I assume someone else's opinions of me are without a shadow of doubt *absolutely* true even when I don't have a shred of proof, or even when I haven't actually *heard* them say anything out loud to me. I just know exactly what they are thinking, because in my mind I'm a real mind reader.

Looney Tunes, right? Who does that? And as if that's not enough, sometimes I feel *fully responsible* for other's emotions, and specifically the happiness of other people—so much so that I twist and turn and bend over backwards to make sure everyone is always okay and no one ever has any yucky feelings ever, because I do not like yucky feelings and am convinced that when they occur it is totally my fault or at least my responsibility to make them unyucky. I have lived a lot of my life less like a human and more like glue holding things together, because with great power (as a super-hero mind reader) comes great responsibility.

Okay. I know. This is just too much. Do we need a break? Or an intervention? Are you somewhat concerned about my mental stability? I hear you, and I just ask that you would have patience, mercy, and grace as I try to untangle this knot that I've just tied us both up in. Unless... oh wait, what's that? You've experienced this exact predicament too? You feel *certain* of what other people think of you, regardless of if they've voiced it or not, and you also feel the weight of the world on your shoulders and never want anyone to feel sad ever, either? Maybe I'm not *loca* after all. Maybe I'm not unusual. Maybe we all do this sometimes.

I can't tell you when I started inhabiting this fantasy world of imaginary opinions and false responsibilities. Maybe it began when, as a child, if I were to open a gift from my grandma, I was instructed to act very, *very* happy, say I loved it (even if I hated it), and, if it happened to be a dress, immediately stop and put it on and do a spin. I never really liked dresses as a kid and I really hated feeling pressured to *absolutely love* something before I even knew what it was—it felt like I was being asked to put on a show so that grandma would be happy. The pressure alone made me not like gifts I may have otherwise liked. I remember once hiding in my bedroom because I refused to come out and show off my new dress to everyone. I am convinced it had little to do with the dress itself and everything to do with the fact that even at a young age, I felt like there was something off about the pressure to please someone just for the sake of making them feel good, particularly when it meant being dishonest.

Obviously, there's nothing wrong with teaching a child to express gratitude, right? And of course that was the conscious effort put forth by my parents—teaching me good manners and gratitude. But I think that beneath the "good manners", from generation to generation, the underlying message passed down is that it is more important to *please people* than to be *honest*.

And that is where the problem lies.

You can be incredibly honest while also being kind. And there would have been absolutely nothing wrong with allowing me, a young girl, to authentically respond to a gift without having to rehearse the situation ahead of time. I think my grandma would have been just fine if, when she were to ask, "Do you like it?", I would have answered honestly, "I think it's great and am so thankful you went out of your way for me! I actually haven't really been wearing dresses lately though." It really doesn't matter as long as it is kind and honest. If grandma would have been offended by kind honesty, well, frankly, that would not have been my problem, it would have been hers. *It is a strange situation when a gift-giver cares more about someone pretending to like it than actually liking it.*

The wiring passed down through generations looks different for everyone. While my brothers were likely being programmed that they ought to produce and provide, I was being programmed to please others. I rarely feel like a failure when I'm not succeeding in something or producing something of value. When I *do* feel like a failure though—when it really cuts deep—is when someone is disappointed in me. In the past, that has rattled me to my core and kept me up at night.

*This* is why we are drowning in the opinions of others. This is why it's so hard to shake. We've been wired since we were little to find the majority of our value in our ability to please other people. If we are pleasing others, we feel a sense (albeit a false sense) of love and belonging.

I am doing everything in my power to have my daughter watch me live free from the prison of other people's opinions, from the incarceration of other's perceptions. I want her to see me living free from false responsibility for others' emotions in hopes that she hardly ever steps foot in that prison cell. If she watches her mama breaking out of it, she might hold herself to that standard and learn that that's not how we do things here. Owning people's emotions is not something we do in our house. We let people feel whatever they are going to feel; the only person responsible for my emotions *is me*, and the only person responsible for my daughter's emotions is my daughter, and so on.

The problem I've found with trying to own someone else's emotions is that it's just like helping your friend cheat on his math homework. If all I'm concerned about is my friend feeling happy and never struggling, then of course, *I'll do your math homework for you!* But come test time, when I see my friend failing his math exam, I'm going to wish I would have encouraged him to work through that homework himself. In other words, owning someone else's emotions and bending over backwards to make sure they never feel anything but sunshine and rainbows is robbing them of the opportunity to grow emotionally. This helps me when I'm feeling tempted to walk on eggshells with someone or move heaven and earth to avoid any yucky feelings. Sometimes being honest and letting someone feel the yucky things is actually the more loving thing to do even if it momentarily feels not so good.

My husband and I have had far too much counseling, both individually and as a couple, to let each other live our lives walking around on eggshells, and we'll do the same for our babies. That means I will allow my daughter to stumble. I will let her figure things out. If she opens a gift from grandma and God forbid, screams every parent's worst nightmare: "This is the worst gift in the world! I hate it and I hate you! Grandma, you suck!", she will deal with the natural consequences of unkind words, and we'll have a talk with her about her behavior. But regardless, I will never coach her to "act happy", and I always teach her that authenticity is far more valuable to the world than anyone's expectations, opinions, or approval of her.

If I'm grounded in whose opinions matter to me, then I won't be tossed and turned by any little thing someone says or thinks of me.

When I'm trying to please other people, what I'm actually doing is trying to "buy love." But if I have to shut down parts of myself or dress myself up in what someone else thinks I should be wearing in order to momentarily feel loved, I'm not actually being loved—what I'm actually doing is tossing away parts of myself. Every time I go quiet or shut down a part of me in order to fit into someone's mold of who they think I should be (or who I *think* they think I should be), I am literally discarding parts of myself. I am disowning pieces of me. I am going to the funeral of my own soul, as pieces of me that deserve a chance to see the light and laugh and dance and sing and speak and breathe freely are being brutally butchered away.

But the truth is that if I am *truly* loved, then I am loved simply because I exist. Because I am a human, because I am worthy of being loved. It has to be that way, because love can't be conditional, it can't be contingent on anything—if it is, it isn't true love. No, it ain't true love, ladies.

Some of the most important, freeing lessons I have learned (and *am* learning) as a woman are these three truths:

I am not *responsible* for the emotions of others. I am responsible for only one person's emotions. Mine.

I am not *defined* by the opinions of others (especially when its not coming from trust and love). I have to dig deep down into my soul and decide who or what is going to define me, but it cannot, for the love of all things holy, be the opinions of other people. That's like anchoring your ship to a moth (1. They can't swim. 2. They have no weight. 3. Like, what are we even thinking here.)

I don't need to please someone in order to be loved by them. I am loved because I am a human being, and for that reason alone. If anyone is making you feel like you have to do more than exist in order to be loved, sister, that is not your people, and that is not real love.

But these aren't the messages we are passing down to one another, generation after generation, are they? So, what does that mean? Do we have centuries of mothers and daughters and grandmas not really loving each other? No. I think we really do love each other. We want nothing more than to love each other, actually. What we don't know how to do is love *ourselves*, and we can only love others out of the overflow of our own hearts. If our hearts are depleted, hungry, and hurting, we will inevitably hurt those closest to us.

"One of the best things we can do to prevent causing pain to others is to begin to feel our own," says therapist and author Hillary McBride. She continues with more gut-punching truth: "Not feeling our pain doesn't just make it go away. It goes somewhere—often into our body, compounding within us, or out against others as we unconsciously try to protect ourselves, cope, or discharge our fear, anger, and sadness. Healing ourselves is part of how we heal the world." But it's so countercultural, isn't it? We are uncomfortable with sadness. We are embarrassed to admit we need counseling. We are told to protect the emotions of others while neglecting our own. But it's precisely the reason we just keep hurting each other. It's the reason we, no matter how much we hated the way our moms talked to us sometimes, find ourselves talking to our daughters the exact same way, whether we want to admit it or not.

There's so much I had to cut loose from, but carrying the weight of other people's emotions or opinions is the one that makes all the other ones so much harder to shake. It's the double-knot you have to loosen before any of the others will budge. We won't heal from our wounds if we don't stop pouring poison into them. We can spend a lifetime healing from our pasts and trying to live authentically in the strength of who God created us to be, but we will constantly have new traumas to heal from. We'll take one step forward and then two steps back when we don't find a way to stop prioritizing other people's opinions of us over authentic living. This includes admitting when we're in pain and addressing that first before trying to heal the rest of the world. Because hurting people hurt people, and if we don't find healing ourselves, we are bound to keep hurting one another. This sounds melodramatic, but, prioritizing the opinions of other people is like poison to our souls, a life-sucking prison. Prisons for approval. Prisons for permission. But we don't need anyone's permission to be true to ourselves, to be free. If we can strip off the need to have everyone's approval or make certain that everyone is always happy, then we can actually start wearing some freedom, and finally start breathing again.

# 9
# Hairy Opinions

There are three kinds of opinions that can haunt us. Confirmed opinions, Unconfirmed opinions, and Confusing opinions. Confirmed opinions are when someone has directly told us something nasty to our face (or our online-face). An unconfirmed opinion is when we're *pretty sure* someone thinks *something*, but don't have concrete proof, and confusing opinions—the hairiest of them all—are, well, *confusing*.

The *confusing opinion* is for those of you who are mind readers, like me. These are the words we are convinced without a shadow of a doubt someone has said about us or believes about us, and even if we don't have *perfect* proof, we have *some* proof.

Maybe we read between the lines, like when your mom observes you mothering your babies, and casually mentions that "When you guys were kids, I did it *this* way instead." She didn't directly tell you, "YOU'RE AN IDIOT FOR DOING IT THAT WAY AND I'M JUDGING YOU." But she also didn't say, "You're doing well, young padawan!" So you are 99.9% certain with your mind-reading abilities that it is hypothetically proven that your mom thinks you're a failure and is judging your every move.

Here's what we can do there, because, well, you can't always just say, "Mom you're being a butthole," and call it a day. You can, however, put on your big girl pants, because now you are speaking to her as an adult and not a young child and challenge her to speak directly instead of passive aggressively. You can remove yourself from the hot seat and instead put her in it and simply ask, "What do you mean by that Mom?" Oh yeah, baby. Let her feel the weight of her loaded statement and let her work through explaining it. Never undervalue the power of posing questions.

Or we can just be really-extra-brave and just tell the truth: "Mom, when you say those types of comments, it makes me feel like you're criticizing the way I am choosing to be a mom. I would prefer you don't say things like that." And that is all you have to say. If she is defensive or chooses to continue being critical, you have spoken your peace, and you might even consider what healthy boundaries with such a critical person look like and not respond anymore. But we either have to be able to let it go and NOT CARE what our moms (or friends, or sisters, or bosses) say, or we have to be willing to tell the truth. But we're not allowed to just stay there stewing on it, feeling bitter, losing sleep over their opinions, or dreading the next time they make us feel deflated.

The opinions and people that make you feel deflated are likely not coming from love (or if there is love for you, it's fogged by their own hurt, fear, or baggage) and just because you decide not to carry it anymore, doesn't mean you're not loving them back. It's actually quite loving to not carry other people's junk for them. In fact, when they see you walking around lighter, it might actually give them permission to let go and carry less too. Freedom is quite a contagious thing.

**Strip Off: Other People's Opinions**

Once we can cut ourselves loose from this one, the rest comes undone more easily. It's like the the double-knot holding all the other strings in place.

**Step Into: Something Risky**

Wear something today that might not be well-received by everyone, which makes it scary. I'm not saying go streaking or moon the next person that drives by your minivan. Just wear something you've always wanted to try but have been hesitant about because of people's opinions.

**GV Fashion Tip**

Sometimes all you have to do to get a little risqué with your outfit is embracing the element of surprise. Try this: mix and match styles—wear something formal with something casual, like a graphic tee with a blazer, or a pair of sneakers with a dress. That's high fashion, baby!

*Dress less to impress and more to express who you truly are.*

# SHAPE SHAME

# 10
# Cankles and Cameltoe

Nothing is funnier than the fact that I've been a personal trainer for the last four years. Now you may not be laughing as you read that, but sister, you have no clue. I'll have you know that I am the *least* naturally athletic human you have ever met in your entire life.

As a kid, moving my body *at all* never came easily to me. I flourished however, in such feats as: spraining my ankle without moving an inch; consuming carbs; flirting with every cute boy within my peripheral vision; and securing just enough C's to graduate. I have never been naturally *athletic*, but I have always been easily *overweight*. I was heavy and unhealthy not only on the scale I'd step on at least twice a day, but on the soul-scale I lived on *all* day long. That scale blinked red with depression, insecurity, and fear. I lived in fear of most things, including exercising on purpose or participating in any activity that required any type of coordination.

I mean, don't get me wrong; I played *all* the sports. All of my friends did, and all of the cutest boys did, so why wouldn't I? But all the fantastic friends and those cute boys couldn't save me from those gym class quarterly fitness exams. There was no glory or getting out of it. I might as well have *died.* Every time.

When I ran cross country in middle school, the agonizing .8 mile run (no, that period is not a typo, it's a legit period) gave me wedgies in places I didn't know were possible, my thighs chafing as they thundered against one another, and as the finish line approached approximately three-and-a-half hours after the race began (at least that's how long it felt), I would drag myself towards the finish line, tears streaking down my cheeks, finishing in 109th out of 110th place. I remember consoling myself after every race, "*Well...I'm not last.*" I did not have high hopes or aspirations when it came to my athletic career.

So, while friends developed devotion to sports and hobbies, I grew in my devotion to carbs. I may not have been an athlete, but when *carbs* were the object of the game, I was a ninja with catlike speed and reflexes. The second my mom cooked rice (which is almost daily in a Cuban household), even if I was in the opposite end of the house, my spidey-sense started tingling and I knew it was go-time. I'd wait until she wasn't looking and then stealthily sneak into the kitchen and scoop an entire fist-full of rice out of the pot with my hand. Did it burn my tiny palm to touch such steamy rice? Absolutely. Did I care? Not one bit. I was so fully committed to my cause: if I had to suffer the sacrifice of a hand, so be it. Instead of singing

"Who stole the cookie from the cookie jar?", my mom would sing, "Who stole the rice from the rice maker?" Well, Mom, it's time you knew. It was me. I stole the rice from the rice maker. Every. Single. Time. Do you know what daily fistfuls of rice gives a middle-schooler wearing a hiked-up uniform? Cameltoe. Cameltoe and shame.

Of course it didn't end in middle school though. In junior high, my teammates all had beautifully sculpted rear-ends and calf muscles that transitioned (as they should) into actual ankles. I on the other hand, just had cameltoe and cankles. The cankles were partially due to my Latina genes sending most of my weight to my lower half, but they were also due to my clumsiness: crutches became a fashion statement for me. Did I actually have chunky ankles, or were they just *always swollen* from spraining them every other day? Who can say? Seriously: one time I twisted my ankle while standing on the *sidelines* during a basketball game. On the sidelines. Who does that?

I say all of this to give you a glimpse into who I was for most of my life. If you're anything like me, part of you believes that happy, healthy, fit people come out of the womb not as squishy wrinkly babies, but as little packages of lean muscle with flexed biceps and perfectly sculpted tushies, and that normal people will never get to experience the fit-folks-life because, well, you can't beat genetics.

And it is true that genetics do play a role in your physical make-up. Unfortunately, I'm pretty sure my genetics left me without a metabolism. Yep, that's right—there are slow metabolisms...and then there's mine. I also think that my genes left me predisposed to hating competition and exerting energy so much that during softball games, I would sit in the grass of left field and play "he loves me, he loves me not" with flower petals as grounders rolled past me. My coach could not, with integrity, even stand to give me a participation ribbon, since "Designated Flower Picker" is simply not a position in softball.

Of course it's all very funny in retrospect, but in reality, I spent so many hours crying in dressing rooms, hating the way I looked, hating my low-energy and low-confidence. Nothing ever fit right and I never really felt right. I would pinch the squish on my stomach and thighs between my hands and think, "If I could just *chop* all this off!" I remember sneaking fat burners from our medicine cabinet in hopes of ridding myself of the unwanted weight.

Hating the way you look is a recipe for depression, at least in my 20+ years of experience. I think in some ways we're all a little predestined to feel depressed at one time or another because of the society we presently live in: at no other time in history have we seen such an excess of photoshopped bodies 24/7 on our phones. Subliminally, these images set the standard for the reflection we see in the mirror every single day. And believe it or not, an excess of photoshopped humans thrust in our faces daily can result in a shortage of serotonin, the "happiness" brain chemical. It doesn't matter how mentally tough I am: if my eyes spend any time taking in pictures of flawless, unrealistic humans, the seconds add up. They add up to minutes. The minutes stream into hours, the hours seep into days, and before you know it we've all sunken into weeks of unhealthy thoughts and comparison.

Before I know it, I have image after image stored up in my mind of all the ways I am not *enough*; all the standards I do not meet. And you know what those thoughts *kindly* deliver to my doorstep? A heck of a lot of the "stress" hormone, cortisol. And when cortisol is hosting a party, he rarely invites serotonin in (happiness, peace, joy). I am not saying our society and social media single-handedly produces a generation of souls lacking happy hormones, but I am saying we're fighting an uphill battle because of it.

Maybe what we're longing for, however, isn't at the top of the hill at all, and we're fighting uphill for nothing.

# 11
# Treasure Isn't Kept On Hills

I worked at multiple gyms and health centers at the start of my career, and my coworkers were some of the most physically fit people I've ever known. They were walking Greek gods with 6% body fat and perfectly sculpted muscles in *allll* the right places. But they were also some of the unhappiest people I'd ever met. It didn't matter how perfect they looked; their focus was always on what they needed to improve. They'd reached the top of the mountain over and over again, and instead of stopping to take in the view, they obsessed over the next highest peak to climb. They were so nitpicky about their bodies that it robbed them of the joy of celebrating what they already had. It made me realize that what I see in the mirror has little to do with how I *actually* look. And what I see in the mirror will never change, no matter how in shape I am, unless I in essence do. And I want you to let those words fill you up, too:

What you see in the mirror will never change, *unless you do.*

I'm not talking about your actual physical reflection, I'm talking about your perception of it. You'll *never* be able to see the beauty—regardless of how fit you get—if you don't start practicing right now. I don't care if you have perfect abs that glisten in the sun as you jog in slo-mo, or if you're on your 253rd round of dieting and you can make homemade Paleo Mayo with your eyes closed. If you look in the mirror and have unkind things to say to yourself or you obsess over certain "trouble" parts of your body, *you are still not healthy.*

For too long, the fitness industry has been shrinking who we are by trying to convince us that a six-pack will make us like ourselves more or be happier, and *it's just not true.* Seeing ourselves as beautiful is NOT something that happens when we finally shed those last 15 pounds, straighten that frizzy hair, or tone up the backs of our arms.

We won't just wake up one morning and finally feel comfortable in our skin; it comes with practice. It's a habit we form, a truth we cultivate, a treasure we hunt for and believe in. That doesn't mean we don't get in shape! It just means we don't wait until we're in shape to love ourselves. In fact, let's get in shape *because* we love ourselves. Any other motivator will result in a never-ending roller coaster of yo-yo dieting and quick-fix 30-day boot camps, ping-ponging between self-hatred and self-obsession, resulting in depression and defeat. It's exhausting and you are worth so much more than that. So let's start hunting for the beauty that's been there all along—it's the one that never fades.

# 12
# How We Hunt

Maybe you're like how I used to be and when someone tells you to "hunt for your beauty" you roll your eyes because it sounds nice in theory. You've heard the same "beauty pitch" a hundred times, and it sounds a whole lot like pie in the sky. It didn't make much sense to me either until I realized I didn't have to figure it out on my own. A counselor I was seeing in my early twenties gave me some hard beauty-hunting homework. The assignment was to ask five people I trust to make a list of what they loved about me, apparently I was rather incapable of coming up with a list on my own, aside from things like "Sometimes I'm nice," or "I'm good at eating tacos."

I was so embarrassed to ask them though, and even apologetic about it. I wanted to say, "Hey you know, it's totally fine if it's a short list. Don't waste too much time on it." But my homework was to *just ask*, and say nothing else.

My five trusted friends made their lists. And I had to sit alone, read them, and pray for God to help me believe their words. I read them over and over again.

If, at first, hunting for your own beauty feels like finding a needle in a haystack (as it did for me), ask your people to help you hunt. And then, have a small handful of things you love about yourself and that others love about you on standby (maybe things like your kind heart, your cute pinky toe, your delightful curves, or your loud and life-giving laughter.) I *know, I know.* These are lame—they won't get you on the cover of Cosmopolitan. They are cheesy. They are self-love bumper-sticker clichés. But they are also the truth. Having an unkind heart is actually a deal-breaker, don't take for granted how special your *kind* one is. Have you ever been around someone *so drop-dead gorgeous*, but their actions or words felt yucky and it was hard to be around them? Humans will always be more drawn in by kindness than by perfection. And internal beauty never fades with age or weight, internal beauty is eternal.

I don't know what you believe about God. I don't want to assume either way, and over the course of the last twelve years I have swung *hard* back and forth between Christian, Agnostic, Atheist, Buddhist, Taco Bell-ist, and that's just to name a few of what I have dabbled with. This is all to say that wherever you're at right now, I'm into it, and I'm into you, honestly. If it wasn't for the people who didn't flinch when I told them "I don't think I believe in God anymore" I don't think I would be where I'm at today. But that's a story for another day. If we're talking about beauty, it's hard for me not to share how my *belief in* and *rela-*

*tionship with* a Creator has actually helped me feel more beautiful, more wanted, and even...wait for it...

More *sexy.*

*Record scratch—um, what? Did she just use the terms "sexy" and "God" in the same sentence? Isn't that against the rules? Isn't that blasphemy?*

It's hard to believe, but if you think God doesn't love when we feel sexy, I invite you to check out a book in the Bible called "Song of Solomon." God is SO into sexy. And so into romance (raise your hand if your pits are sweaty at the idea of sexy spirituality!)

God? Into *romance*? Oh, what a coincidence, I was basically bred on Romantic Comedies. I can speak this language.

One of my favorite things to keep ready in my pocket is the idea that God is *giddy* about me, even on my ugliest days—giddy like Romeo was for Juliet, or Jack was for Rose, or Troy Bolton was for Gabriela. He sings over me because of how much He loves me (like, break-out-into-song-in-the-middle-of-the-school-cafeteria-style). *He sings over me when I don't have the strength to sing.* And even on my ugliest days, God is head-over-heels for me. In chapter three of the book of Zephaniah in the Bible, things get *real* romantic: "The LORD your God is in your midst, a mighty one who will save; he will rejoice over you with gladness; he will quiet you by his love; he will exult over you with loud singing." You know how in rom-coms the cute guy is totally head-over-heels in love and willing to make a fool out of himself and sing sappy love-song-serenades at his lady's window loud enough to wake the neighbors? This is what I picture when I read that verse. Again, there is no pressure here to believe what I do. But I think there's a Creator who is head-over-heels for you, serenading you, because you're just *that* worth it. You are that beautiful. That wanted. That sexy.

Just imagine if you believed every single one of those things: you are beautiful, wanted, and sexy, head to toe, heart, mind, and soul. If you never doubted your beauty or worth and you knew down to your core that God was giddy about you, how would you stand, walk, and talk?

Remember, finding your beauty is a choice, not something we leave to chance for "one day" when we're finally where we want to be. Let your body language and speech reflect that choice.

Now when I'm in a room full of people and I feel the shrinking begin, feel myself shutting down, or believing that I'm not wanted, I adjust my posture. I remember that feeling beautiful isn't something I just feel or do, it's something I *choose*. So I let my body language reflect that choice. I stand up straight. I speak even if my voice is shaky, or if my cheeks get red, I speak even if I have to try three times before I stop getting cut off by the more outspoken one in the room. I speak until someone actually hears me. It isn't "faking it 'til I make it", it's choosing a posture that believes in the beauty and worth God put in me, even if I don't "feel" it in the moment. With enough practice, my mind starts to observe and mimic my posture, I start believing it, and I even start feeling it.

It's also worth noting that when we compare ourselves to women on screens (TV, Instagram, Facebook, etc.), we aren't comparing ourselves to everyday humans. Did you know that fitness models or instructors will often hardly eat anything right before a shoot so that they have an insanely low (and unhealthy) body fat percentage? This way, they look extra fit and lean...for 24 hours. None of them walk around in their day-to-day lives looking the way they lead you to believe they do. We *have* to stop comparing ourselves to unreal humans. It's the reason body shaming is so common—these quick, drastic body fat cuts celebrities do for filming or photo shoots leave us with impossible standards. So when the one brave celebrity *doesn't* do this and God-forbid we see a fraction of jiggle in her belly as she dances on stage, the whole world erupts with hysteria at the sight of her healthy "gut". UGH. Give me a BREAK. If our standard of beauty is based on a woman who doesn't exist in real life, how will we ever feel beautiful?

Let's choose a physical posture that is consistent with the beauty we are choosing to believe in, because loving the skin we're in is a mindset we hunt for, not a body we work for.

## 13
# A Friggin' Wonderland

As I type these words out, I'm a million miles in the air on route to Vancouver, Canada for the most ridiculous reason. Last week when it was that *special* time of the month when rational thoughts are hard to come by, I was laying in bed crying because in those two-and-a-half minutes I was convinced I was the greatest failure to ever walk the earth, that no one likes me, and I would never be not bloated ever again in my life. I was listening to a sad song (as you do when you decide to really dig in your heels and stay a while in your sadness) and my sweet friend Lana, who also just happens to be a famous movie star, facetimed me. I almost didn't answer because an #uglycrying face is not a cute facetime face. But since we were friends before she was all famous and movie-star-y and she's already seen me cry seventy-five million times, I figured it was safe.

"Awww, Gelly. I'm sorry it's been a hard day, girl. You're amazing and not a failure. Also, I have some news that might cheer you up! What are you doing next week-end?"

Now. When you hear the words, "News that might cheer you up" and "What are you doing next weekend" come out of a famous person's mouth, you start hyperventilating, because you can never be sure what's about to happen next. Are we having lunch with Michelle Obama? Taking selfies by the Eiffel Tower with champagne, puppies in our hands, and organic cucumbers over our eyes? What do famous people even do "next weekend"?!?

As I tried to stop hyperventilating, Lana went on: "H&M is contracting me to do their holiday line photo shoot and they asked me to pick a friend to fly up here to be in the shoot with me. And I immediately thought of you!"

It felt like my actual heart fell out of my butt. WHAT?! Me?! In a photo shoot with YOU?! For THEM?!? I just sat with my mouth open in shock and then kept repeatedly yelling, "What is happening?! Wait. WHAT ARE YOU EVEN SAYING RIGHT NOW?" It was all just too much: being flown out of the country, getting six hours of time on a plane where I could read and write and do whatever-the-heck-I-wanted-and-wipe-precisely-ZERO-toddler-butts, for the purpose of getting to be in an eight hour shoot with one of my dearest friends? Too. Much. I thought about it for nearly half of a millisecond and proceeded to give her a teary-eyed "YES! I'm so in."

She sent over a list of questions I had to answer for the stylist who was setting up the shoot.

Before we go on, let's be clear about something. I have devoted so much of my work to a healthy body image for myself and to empowering other women to take what the fitness industry and social media feeds us on a daily basis, and turn it upside-down. I am a personal trainer for crying out loud; a personal trainer who practically never weighs herself because she believes that the number on the scale is essentially meaningless, because healthy, strong women will always weigh a little more because muscle weighs more than fat. We all know this. I know this. I believed it so fully and had absolutely no reason to give even the smallest rip about what I weighed.

But when I went to measure my height and weight for the stylist, something bizarre happened.

I weighed myself with my laptop open next to me, ready to send the email; 122.3 pounds. It was a super healthy weight for my height and I didn't think much about it. Remember, after a lifetime of battling my weight (in many seasons weighing 40 or 50 pounds more than I did in that moment), and four years of being a personal trainer, I didn't care a whole lot about the scale anymore.

But then I went to write it down. And here is how my thoughts unraveled into utter *ridiculousness* in a matter of milliseconds:

*Cool, 122.3! Let me just jot that down. Well, hold up a*

*sec. 122.3 is an annoying number. Who sends such an uneven number? [*Quickly finding logic and scientific basis for my thoughts*] I mean, 122 is fantastic for me, REALLY; everything is awesome. But what do models weigh? What kind of numbers do they normally send in? Will they read 122.3 and think I'm not model material? I should just round to the nearest ten. 122 is basically 120 anyway. It's just two pounds (and a half) for crying out loud. I'm not lying, right? And who knows, maybe after a good poop I actually would be about 120. It's not uncommon to fluctuate 1-2 pounds throughout a day. So yeah, I should write down 120.*

IMMEDIATELY after pressing send I felt gross; like I had just been possessed with thoughts that didn't sound like me. In that moment, when it all came rushing at me—what I had done, and how societal demands for us to be something we aren't, *smaller* than we are, can creep in so subtly, I wished I would have rounded UP to 125 *just because*. Because maybe when we do the shoot, I will have just eaten the best burrito Vancouver has to offer. Because NO, I am not a model in real life and I won't pretend to be on paper either. Also BECAUSE I CAN and BECAUSE MY BODY IS A FRIGGIN' WONDERLAND regardless of your devil numbers and sizes. Listen here, fancy media people, you will take a picture of me in all my non-model glory and you will *like it*. Also I will probably talk about bodily functions or something else ridiculous to break the ice, which I am also guessing your models don't typically do. And hopefully you will laugh at it. Or never hire me again; that's cool too. Either way, I'm gonna keep doin' me in my non-traditional model-who-loves-tacos glorious life.

I know that numbers are a sensitive topic, but please hear me here. It was NOT about the numbers. The point is that even at an incredibly healthy weight (and as a health coach, for crying out loud), I was still faced with the temptation to round the number down. We can all fall into the trap that says a smaller number is better or more beautiful. But that is just not the case. The number on the scale has NOTHING to do with anything. At my healthiest physical state when I was lifting more, I weighed ten pounds heavier, and it was awesome. What if instead of stepping on our scales every morning we stepped into truth instead?

Well, when it was all said and done, they were all actually SUPER cool, down-to-earth people. And those were all standards I was assuming they'd have and not something they ever communicated to me. I was super honored to be part of such a fun experience with lots of talented, kind people. (And yes they did laugh at my ridiculous icebreakers about bodily functions.)

But do you SEE how quickly and subtly those

thoughts of not-enough or too-much creep in? The subtle art of shrinking ourselves in order to make someone else approve of us is so smooth and sneaky that we never see it happening, even when it's right in front of us. EVEN when we've devoted a career against it.

I have felt so liberated from body image struggles for so long and have even helped coach other women to feel the same way, and YET, in a matter of milliseconds, I felt the pressure from society and from myself to be and look a certain way, I compared who I really am to who I thought "they" wanted me to be, and I wrote something down that was *untrue enough* to do myself a disservice. The two pound difference wasn't the point; it really doesn't matter or make a difference. The wild part was the idea that I could ever squeeze into someone's tiny box or unrealistic expectations of me. That will never happen.

I will never please enough people.

I will never be everyone's cup of tea.

I will never be a long-legged slender model with 0% body fat.

It's wildly untrue that we could ever meet the standards of our society in our natural form. So if it's wildly untrue, then trying to live up to it is wildly insane. It's as if we were trying to hit a bullseye with an arrow but the target was just a mirage—we're shooting for something that *literally* doesn't exist, and we're wasting our precious energy and entire life by shooting for it over and over and over again.

Let's put the bow and arrow down, and walk forward, straight through that target mirage, blowing past it and with no looking back. Your body is a friggin' wonderland, girl.

14

# My Body is a Wonderland. There. I Said it, and I'm Not Sorry.

One of my favorite psychologists, Hillary McBride, focuses her life's work on body image and women. She's expressed that an overwhelming *98% of women would say that they hate their bodies.* NINETY-EIGHT PERCENT, you guys. That's so freaking sad I want to bawl my eyeballs out when I hear it. But, like most statistics and studies, there's more to the story.

McBride realized that there is extensive research on women who *hate* their bodies, but, surprisingly, there is little to no research on women who *love* their bodies. So she decided to conduct her own research on women who love their bodies. When she requested for volunteers for the study, she was assuming that hardly anyone would respond because there's practically no one out there who actually *does* love her body. But surprisingly, she was overwhelmed by the amount of women that responded. In a nutshell, what she came to find was that because the body hatred narrative is so ingrained in our society, the women who *do* love their bodies feel isolated and outcast from connection with other women because they can't relate or chime in on the body hatred conversation. They fear they won't be understood, and they fear that their love for their bodies will at *best* make their sisters feel bad about their own bodies, and at *worst*, they'll be considered vain.

Sisters, we can do better than this. We *have* to do better than this. If we don't create freedom and space for a new narrative about our bodies, nothing will ever change. So I'll go ahead and say this: You are allowed to love your body. And you are allowed to tell your sister you love your body and not feel anxious about how she'll feel because of it. Whether or not she hears that and assumes it must mean her body is lacking *is not on you.* Perhaps your freedom to verbalize approval, love, and self-compassion for your body will give her permission to love hers as well. What if one conversation at a time we changed the narrative, together? What if on shopping trips we challenged each other to look in the mirror and hunt for beauty about ourselves instead of nitpick? We are so incredibly complex, gifted, and talented, and there is so much more we can connect on aside from body hatred.

# 15
# The Magic

I know that this section of the book will make my loved ones sad. Specifically my mom, my dad and my best friend, Danielle.

My dad will be bummed because he really was the most affirming and loving that a father can be. I remember once asking him during some of my chubbier years, "Daddy, does this make me look fat?" And he'd gently respond with something like, "You look absolutely beautiful! I mean sure, you could be healthier, but we all could! And that has absolutely nothing to do with how beautiful you are." What a kind yet honest way to answer such a hard question.

My mom will be sad because she always told me I was beautiful. She never nitpicked. And she's right; she never said a word to me that would have made me feel anything but beautiful. However, what she didn't realize (and what I think most of us don't realize as mothers) is that our eyes say more than most words can—especially when we're looking in the mirror. I saw disappointment in my mom's face when she looked at herself in the mirror. I even remember seeing her play with flab on her belly or arms. She didn't nitpick *my body* once, but I saw how her eyes tore her own body apart, and that's far more profound than almost anything for a daughter. If you see my mom though, you would think she's absolutely crazy for ever looking in the mirror and seeing anything but jaw-dropping beauty. She really is the kind of beauty that makes your head turn, even as a grandmother.

And my best friend Danielle was one of the most athletic girls in our school. She encouraged me to get in the game and never got mad if I missed our winning shot. She was competitive, yet she never made me feel less than for dragging our team down. She said reading these words made her sad because all she ever saw in me growing up was beauty and joy and silliness. She never once saw me as a chubby little girl who came in last during our cross country races (even as she almost always came in first). Even then, it was true—we just don't see ourselves the way others see us. Even the people we think ought to most easily love themselves never do.

So if you find yourself thinking, *if I just had so-and-so's body, I'd be happy, I would love myself,* well, sister, chances are so-and-so feels the same way about some other so-and-so.

# 16
# Oh, Hey Mama

In my prime as a personal trainer, one of my main clientele groups was moms. Understandably so; we juggle so many things at once that to have someone lead us through how to get healthy, and in a way, take something off our plate, is incredibly helpful. I was all about working with moms. However, I started to get weary when I kept having moms reach out to me who had babies 45-seconds-old asking me how they could lose the baby weight. Since I kept having the same conversation over and over again, I wrote out a program I could give to all moms who had newborn babies. It went a little something like this:

Step 1: Stop reading this and go take a nap.

Step 2: Ask your neighbor to come over and take your trash out.

Step 3: Get in proper squat stance, and lower your butt down, down , down...until both cheeks are comfortably pancaked onto your couch (bonus points if you still have hemorrhoids from pushing out an entire human and need a pillow in addition to the couch.)

Step 4: Turn on "This is Us" and therapeutically cry for the next seven hours straight while feeding your baby.

Step 5: STOP WORRYING ABOUT THE BABY

WEIGHT. Enjoy the fullest breasts you've ever had and keep rocking your maternity clothes. You look hot. Some women pray for the stretch marks you hate yourself for.

Step 6: Drink your Uncle Larry's weight in ounces of water. Then start the Whole30 diet. Get three hours in to Day One, then realize your brain isn't working enough to read a recipe and will continue to not work for the next three months. You can try again then.

Step 7: Repeat steps 1-3, and then go on a walk (optional.)

Step 8: Go buy jeans that actually fit this weird limbo stage you're in instead of torturing yourself for not yet fitting into your pre-baby jeans or your 9-month maternity jeans.

Step 9: Get on the floor and have the best intentions of doing yoga for twenty minutes; enjoy the first 2.5 minutes of cat cow and down dog, and then pause the DVD because your baby woke up and needs to eat. Finish the dvd later that month.

Step 10: Once your baby is three months old, THEN we can *maybe* talk about a traditional workout plan. Until then, become a master of steps 1-9. You need sleep in order for your muscles to even recover from a workout, and you're not going to sleep for the next three months *at least*, so just CHILL. Your baby is developing their self-esteem starting from day one as they observe the way you treat yourself, so be kind, patient, and loving to yourself.

Mothers get the worst of it though, honestly. It can be so hard to be kind, patient, and loving to ourselves because we are shamed into believing there's a certain time frame where we've got to get our shiz together post-baby. And in practically any scenario, it is impossible to be kind, patient, or loving when we feel rushed. We are given a thousand and one programs for getting our "pre-baby body back", but what drives me absolutely bananas is this: Imagine if we were told by insurance companies that in *30 days or less we can have our pre-baby insurance plan back*. We would be offended, wouldn't we? We want this precious life covered by insurance and safe. Or what if our baby-free friends demanded we be just as available as we were before we became parents? We would be offended if the people around us were constantly pushing or advertising things to us in such a way that undermined or dismissed the beautiful addition to our family, even alluding to them not existing at all. Yet, as mothers we want every other part of our life to embrace this *new life* except our bodies—we want *those* to bounce right back and act like nothing ever happened.

So here's what I've been telling myself. I don't want a pre-baby *life*, so I don't want a pre-baby *body*. I want the body that spent every night holding my daughter and singing to her under the stars that kissed my skin as I kissed hers. I want *this* body; the one with all the stories told through scars like whispers. I want the body that grew and sustained a human. Or even if you didn't carry your babies, it's *your* body that they find comfort in. It's the body that held them through fevers and nightmares and heartbreaks. I want *that* body, because it's the body of a warrior. Strong and beautiful.

It's not that we stop caring and let ourselves go, it's that we stop comparing ourselves to *the me I used to know.* And the thing is, it's only when I stop wishing for the body I *had* that I can actually take care of the body I *have.* And I won't drop the weight until I drop the shame and the worship of the past.

Mama, who you are is exactly the mother your kids need. They don't need that other mom that has it all together, they need *you*. Regardless of how put-together or hot-mess-express you feel today, you are a freaking drop-dead-gorgeous warrior mama from your head to your toes. Now pour yourself a glass of wine, it's been a long day. Cheers!

17
# Easy Breezy

For a long time, I assumed I would finally be able to love myself *easily* when I reached a certain weight, size, complexion, tone, etc. I thought it would be easy to love myself when all of those ducks were in a row. But what I came to learn was that even those people who I saw as "easily loveable" (gorgeous, funny, in shape, successful) still didn't love themselves fully: they, like everyone else, only saw flaws and battled insecurities. So I started realizing that the important work wasn't in becoming *easily loveable* but becoming a *fully loved* person, and that had to start with my capacity to truly love myself fully, *with* all my flaws. Even when it's hard. If spirituality is your sort of thing, here is where I'd say self-love comes out of fully grasping how much my Creator loves me, regardless of flaws. I love myself fully: not easily, but fully. Do you see the difference? Full love takes work. It loves, *really* loves regardless of the weather, the mood, the weight. Easy love is a fantasy; it's conditional. It says, "I love you *if*", and that, by definition, is not love.

And that, my friends, wraps up the self-love conversation. Just, like, *accept yourself*, man. Make a decision to love yourself and everything will be a walk in the park from now on. You won't see any more flaws when you look in the mirror. Just, choose harder. Mean it more. Do better.

Wait, you're thinking that's easier said than done?

WOMP WOMP.

Yep, you're totally right; this thing is a daily battle, and we will all still have hard days. Hard days when we have to remind ourselves that full, unconditional love is better than easy, conditional love.

What's really fun is the fact that fully loving myself is the *only* state where I am even able to get healthy. For most of my life it was pretty normal for my weight to fluctuate constantly up-and-down 10 to 15 pounds, and that's not including the seasons when I was about 40-50 pounds overweight long-term. Funnily enough, though, I stopped dramatically fluctuating in my weight after I had been going to counseling for a while. When I first started trying to understand what truly loving myself meant, I just started walking every day to have time to myself, for myself. Walking was therapy for me; at the time I would walk four to eight miles a day just listening to music and breathing. I wasn't moving because I wanted to torture my body or force it into shape, I was moving because I was finding freedom and healing in movement.

When moving my body came out of self-love instead of self-hate, I actually started to lose weight.

About a month ago, I actually told my last two clients that I would be retiring from being a personal trainer indefinitely. There were a few different reasons I did it but one of them was that it became increasingly difficult for me to assign exercise routines to people when what I wanted to tell them was to fall in love with movement. To fall in love with self-care out of compassion and not out of desperation, to fall in love with being alive...that's not something you can package up and sell very easily. Most clients wanted me to tell them how to focus on losing weight around their belly (or other specific "trouble" body parts), or to give them the perfect ab exercise routine, or the perfect formula in order to look a certain way. That's like asking me to put a band-aid over an infected gash in your leg; it's just not that simple. And sure, I could have given them a quick-fix answer; some new diet program or routine to give them temporary results, but the reality is that it doesn't matter how perfect your nutrition or workout program is: if it's not fueled by self-love instead of an obsession with flaws, it won't last. I felt my integrity throw up a white flag of surrender. I didn't want to sell band-aids anymore if we weren't also giving attention to the deeper wound, the root issue.

Unconditional love is the key, I promise. Because unconditional love gives space for mistakes instead of shame from mistakes, and shame is the least productive thing a person could ever feel. Shame says, "You suck anyway, just eat the whole bag of donuts." Shame says, "I'll start tomorrow. Today is a lost cause." Shame says, "I am disgusted with myself." Shame says, "I'll only let you fly when you're worthy," and our bodies respond back, "I won't ever be enough for you, so why try?"

We've been allowing our pursuits of health to be dictated by a *shame* narrative instead of a *space* narrative.

Embracing a space narrative means making room for errors so that when they inevitably occur you can respond with love and with a plan of action rooted in compassion instead of spiraling out of control in disgust, shame, or disappointment. It's giving your body permission to take its most natural, healthy form; its *own* best shape, instead of obsessing over someone else's best shape and trying to fit into that.

# 18
# The Best Workout Plan

You might think that as a former personal trainer I would consider including a healthy, balanced workout plan in the section of my book on body image, right? I mean, clearly I believe in taking care of our bodies, and I will talk about what my workouts have looked like in a later chapter—how I trained for a half marathon, how I love lifting weights, and how I adore yoga and dance. Having a healthy conversation about exercise and the fitness industry doesn't mean I think working out (or even wanting to look and be fit as a whole) is bad. That's not what I'm saying at all. I just don't think conversations about getting fit belong in this section. I talk about these things later on in the context of getting out of my comfort zone out of LOVE for myself—out of knowing that there is great benefit in challenging my body to move—but it needs to be a completely separate conversation from our body image and how we learn to love ourselves. It needs to have nothing to do with the space narrative.

The space narrative says we move, correct, or discipline not in order to *be* loved, but *out of* love. On the days when my head is on straight and I am disciplining my daughter with intention, before correcting her I will often say, "I love you so much no matter what," because I don't want her to think that her bad decision makes her whole self bad or unloved. The fact that she is adored can not change no matter what she does, and we can treat ourselves with this same unconditional love. The space narrative says, "Oh, you were on a nutrition cleanse but you went to this birthday party and had a couple bites of chocolate cake when you weren't thinking? That's ok, dear, you're only human, and you're loved regardless. Your next bite of food will be something you choose on purpose because you believe you're worth good fuel. Better yet, let's walk away from the food table and go talk to that person that makes us laugh—that dopamine is even better than the one the chocolate cake gave you, I promise." When I correct myself via the space narrative, there is love and compassion.

The space narrative also doesn't spiral out of control, because it's operating out of self-compassion. Space is *grace*, whereas shame is *condemnation*. Shame says, "I CAN'T BELIEVE I ATE THAT STUPID CAKE THAT WASN'T EVEN GOOD. DANGIT. Now my cleanse is RUINED, just like I am. I am RUINED. A lost cause. I will try again next month." The space narrative gently corrects us in our thinking that the "all or nothing" motto ought to be sent back to where it was born—the pit of hell. I KNOW that's dramatic, but I'm serious. The all or nothing mentality, which is the mentality I lived on for essentially all my life, is the pendulum swinging between "I am perfect" and "I am disgusting." It's the reason we all fluctuate back and forth in weight and health so much. We are either on top of a mountain as triumphant queens, or we are in the deepest valley with our face buried in the dirt, unworthy of eating the dog's scraps. This has to stop.

I may not ever have super-ripped biceps the way I once did, or that perfect teardrop quad muscle in the front of my leg, but my heart is in good shape because I run around outside with my daughter and our dog and dance with my family in the kitchen as we cook dinner: a delicious, nutritious meal that serves us well and makes our hearts and bellies happy and that says to our bodies, "You have everything you need to fly; I love you, take this fuel and soar, baby!"

And out of care for my body, instead of destroying myself with an all-or-nothing grind of a workout plan, I have learned proper exercise methods so that when I lift weights or go for a run, I strengthen my core and my muscles and my joints instead of throwing out my back.

It's such a subtle but life-altering perspective shift.

Again, I am not saying working out is bad, or that planned programs aren't sometimes excellent tools to aid in our health journeys. I am just saying I think sometimes they are a bandaid we put over an infected wound and then get mad when we never really heal. The magic, though, is in making a lifestyle out of mindfulness and movement because we are loved *as we are.*

Oh, and for the record? I don't have cankles. I am rebuking that self-belief in the name of Jesus. You know what I have? I have two ankles that are attached to my feet. My ankles work really freaking hard for me all day, and I don't care if their ratios aren't petite enough for some designer's skinny jeans; they serve every purpose I need them to, and I adore them.

**Strip Off: Shape Shame**

"The curious paradox is that when I accept myself as I am, then I can change."

- Carl Rogers

**Step Into: Something Gentle**

Wear something today that is comfortable, cozy, and still feels cute. Maybe it's a sweater that brings back happy memories. Maybe it's your most forgiving jeans (who are we kidding, don't wear real pants today. Pull those sweats out!) Something easy. Something soft that sits on your skin just perfectly. It's not something you have to adjust every few seconds or check in the mirror to see how it looks. Once it's on, I want you to look in the mirror and with that same softness that you feel this outfit has for you, love yourself just as gently. If you're feeling brave, you can even say something like, "I love you no matter what," as you look in the mirror. Maybe you even write that on the mirror so you can remember it tomorrow. Give yourself some unconditional love.

**GV Fashion Tip**

I am recently loving mom-jeans, boyfriend-jeans, and your grandma's-jeans that I find at Goodwill and cut up and shape to my liking. The thing I love about all of these options is how baggy and comfortable they are—it almost feels like I'm wearing sweatpants with them on (#BLESS.) The trick with baggy pants is cutting or folding them up high enough so that a little bit of ankle peeks through. If you've got some ankle showing, you can go as baggy as your heart desires and you still won't feel frumpy.

*The mirror will always confirm whatever I already believe about myself. When I step into love, that's when I see my beauty, not the other way around. Also, dang, I've got some sexy ankles.*

# RE-RUNS

# 19
# Re-Runs

A few months ago we sold our TV.

It wasn't just any TV either.

It was a SMART TV roughly the size of a small car. It curved. It had an extendable, rotating wall mount so that if I so desired, I could angle it toward the kitchen and watch *New Girl* reruns while cooking dinner. Oh, and it was also a gift.

So we sold a big amazing TV that we got for *free*.

Maybe at this point you're telling yourself, *Oh, surely they sold the TV in order to replace it with an even better one!* I mean, we aren't savages, and we aren't Amish, so that would be a perfectly reasonable assumption.

However.

To this day, now three months later as I write this, there's still just a white wall where the TV was once mounted. We didn't replace it with a bigger or better TV, or even a smaller, less awesome TV for that matter, and we haven't even decorated the wall. It's just a blank canvas waiting for me to make up my mind about what I want there. Our house isn't huge, so having such a gigantic TV in a central room of the house made the TV the focal point. And it started to bug me. My daughter, too young to talk but old enough to know how to work the remote (which has always freaked me out), adored that TV. And by "adored" I mean she transformed into a raging psychopath when we wouldn't let her watch it. Not only were my daughter's tantrums increasing in intensity surrounding the TV, but we also realized we didn't actually like the way our time watching TV made us feel.

We would be exhausted from a long day, and then without thinking we would turn on Netflix and start watching our favorite shows. We were on our third round of *New Girl* and our second round of *Parks and Rec*, and we were soaking up the last beautiful moments of *Friends*.

The tricky part with watching TV shows—especially on a streaming platform like Netflix—is that you have only 15 seconds to pivot after each episode. One foot is rooted in exhaustion and disregard of any bit of adult responsibility, and the other foot is your one chance to make an honorable decision. Do you know how many good decisions I've been able to make when I'm tired and given only 15 seconds? None. No good decisions whatsoever. I need at least 45 seconds minimum to work things out in my head. I mean, you've been there before right? You decided to watch just one show, just one episode after the baby went down. After that ONE show, you'd work on a project, clean the kitchen, read a book so your brain doesn't melt into a puddle before your eyes, or, God forbid, just go to bed early like a civilized person who works the next day. But that one episode ends and by the time your conscious self actually realizes what's happening, you've already lost five seconds, now leaving you with just ten precious seconds to decide your next step. You look at the episode to come, and it's a shorter one, only a measly 27 minutes long, which is essentially nothing, and hey, you can brush your teeth while you watch, and let the dog out (remember, your TV rotates, so anything is possible.) So, like any good multitasker, you decide you should really just let it play. You made so many good decisions today, like, for example, not throwing your toddler out a window, so you can let this one slide and watch just one more episode.

Three hours later, all hope is lost. Even the dog is staring at you, his black eyes judging you for binging.

We spent enough days dealing with tantrums and enough nights falling into a Netflix black hole that we just decided to get crazy and sell the dang thing. We had nothing to lose (besides, you know, a big TV.) Plus, as emergency backup, we had a small TV in storage that we figured we could hook up if we really wanted to later on.

Well it's been about three months, and I know we'll sound like crazy hippies when I tell you this, but we haven't even missed it. We've spent our evenings snuggled up in bed reading books, or working on projects, or hanging out with people we love, or making love (huzzah!), or writing, or just sitting and chatting while we drink tea. I mean, I *feel* crazy as I write it. But it made me realize that so much of our time was spent re-living episodes we had already seen or hoping someone would put out a new episode we loved that we stopped doing things that *actually* give us life. Watching TV every once in a while is still absolutely cozy and delicious when we snuggle up with the laptop in bed or something, but the binging shows or defaulting to it every night kept leaving us feeling stagnant and actually less rejuvenated, less rested. We thought unplugging and turning our brains off was what we needed to rest, but *plugging in* to the moment has actually felt so much more restful.

Now, this actually has nothing to do with TV. I am sure when Jane the Virgin comes back on in a few weeks, I will want to plug in that little TV and obsessively wait for every new episode like I am 15 years-old and it is the most important part of my day.

But what I am learning with this new blank wall in my house where the TV used to be is that, just like so many of our nights defaulted to watching reruns, so many of the spaces in my mind are just reruns, too. They are the realities from my past, that I, without realizing, allow to

play over and over again, like the Netflix show that just
never turns off or gives me enough time to pivot.

# 20
# Stuck On Loop

A friend of mine adopted her son out of foster care. When he was dropped off at their house by a caseworker at 9 P.M., he had 26 bruises and two black eyes. No human, no matter their age, should ever ever, *ever* experience that kind of abuse…but you guys, he was *one.* ONE. YEAR. OLD. It still makes me sick to my stomach every time I think about it.

Because of that trauma, her son's brain froze in time as a coping mechanism. Even though he is now five, there are areas of his brain that show no further development than an infant's brain. You can imagine how difficult that makes things for all of them as it affects his behavior and capacity to process things and function normally.

Obviously this is an extreme case, but I think any trauma does this to us in varying degrees. Somewhere in the corners of our mind, we get stuck in whatever was happening and however old we were when we experienced the trauma.

Now, I don't want you to read this and think, *Well I wasn't brutally beaten; I've had a decent life, and the pain I've experienced wasn't that traumatic, therefore, I must not have any areas in my brain that are "stuck" because it just wasn't that bad.* But friends, trauma cases aren't exclusive to those of us whose lives could be the plot in a horror film. In fact, trauma creates its own haunted house of sorts in the brain: the kind that makes us stay as far away from reflecting on our emotions as possible. Trauma is defined as what happens when natural neural pathways in the brain are broken due to distress that the mind or body cannot handle. Put more simply, trauma is an interruption in the frequencies of our brain. Emotional, physical, spiritual; it doesn't matter what method the blow came in—if it stopped us in our tracks and forced our brain into a protective fight or flight state, there's some degree of trauma. Your trauma may have been "only" as intense as an overbearing mom that made you feel like nothing you did was ever good enough, or it may have been a severe assault. Dr. Gabor Mate, a specialist in childhood trauma, explains it perfectly:

> *When people see this word [trauma], they often—perhaps naturally—assume that we are speaking of terrible events, such as abuse, sexual exploitation, the death of parents, violence in the home, and so on. And surely, as the research abundantly shows, the more such experiences a child has to endure, the exponentially greater his or her risk of addiction. But trauma is not restricted to horrific experiences. It refers to any set of events that, over time, impose more pain on the*

> *child than his or her sensitive organism can process and discharge. Therefore, trauma can occur not only when bad things happen, but also when the parents are too stressed, too distracted, too depressed, too beset by economic worry, too isolated, etc. to respond to a sensitive child's emotional need to be seen, emotionally held, heard, validated, made to feel secure. Such is the reality behind many a story of "happy childhood." In fact, the denial of one's pain, the splitting off of distress from conscious memory, is one of the outcomes of trauma.*

The point is, we *all* have stuff that's stuck, and we won't heal from our pain if we are always comparing it to others' or making it smaller than it is. Your pain is yours and yours alone, and no one gets to tell you how it's supposed to feel or if you are feeling it too deeply. The sooner we start to feel safe enough to feel things fully, the sooner we will stop hating how we feel all the time. But sometimes people who are deeply traumatized don't actually know where to even start when it comes to identifying their emotions, let alone really feeling them. It's like asking them to enter that haunted house, or at least that's how it felt to me. That being said, I've lived for years as a divided person, with pieces of my mind stuck on loop, racked with re-runs. I've battled depression, anxiety, PTSD, panic attacks, and debilitating social anxiety. For so long I just thought I was a file in a doctor's cabinet with a laundry list of diagnoses under my name and a mountain of prescription pills prescribed to me. And while there were so many different factors playing in to this, a huge part of it all was that my brain was stuck playing reruns.

I had gone through some counseling, but so many of the counselors just saw my diagnosis, my illness. So many of the psychologists just approached my treatment with symptom relief, giving me mental band-aids but ignoring the infected wounds beneath. And it wasn't until the last four years that I finally started seeing counselors who were less concerned with my symptoms and more concerned with what was going on in my brain and soul that were causing them. They began walking with me through whole healing from the inside out, and I started realizing that so many of my *current* struggles were my brain's attempts to cope with things from my past.

# 21
# Monsters Under My Bed

The earliest I remember being depressed was on Sundays.

Every Sunday at about 4 PM, I would pack my little plastic Walmart bag with the essentials—my favorite pair of jeans, a book I was unrealistically optimistic about finishing, a journal, and my walkman. With pits in our bellies, my brothers and I would leave one parent's house and get dropped off at the other's.

Every week this was our routine, from when I was eight years old until about seventeen. Back and forth, every Sunday at 4, and not a minute later or *someone* would remind *everyone* about the custody agreement. Our parents didn't realize it made us feel like cattle getting shipped from one barn to the next, like a business transaction.

Listen: I have two of the most incredible parents a girl can dream of having. But that doesn't mean that, when they were incredibly hurt by each other, no one else was affected by the fallout of their broken relationship. It's just how life works, and I am sure that in my own pain, I too, have caused someone else pain.

It never really got easier, either. Every Sunday was a little death: a death to my hopes for a normal family; a breeding ground for my envy of children with only one sock drawer, one bed, one family, one set of rules. I was also *always* losing things and jealous of the kids who had ONE house to search when something went missing, because I had two houses to search, along with lots of half-ripped open Walmart bags that I lived out of.

I can still only recall *two* memories from childhood B.D. (before divorce)—otherwise, my mind is completely void of any memories whatsoever (I'm working on getting more of those memories back and redeeming them, but more on that later.) Sometimes I've asked my best friend Danielle to tell me what it was like to see my parents married, because she has more memories of them together than I do. It's as if I was born an eight year-old. Trauma has a way of doing that to you: stripping reality from you and layering darkness and confusion in its place. There are spaces in my brain that have been stuck playing re-runs from when I was eight—associations, triggers, belief systems, or memories stuck in a twilight zone loop that have been hard for me to reflect on or break out of.

My parents did their very best to transition us well. I'm told we attended a few family counseling sessions, complete with crayon-illustrated emotions and "It's Not Your Fault" kid comic pamphlets. And each of my parents had their own way of discussing the divorce with us, wanting to ease the blow. But the hardest part about divorce is that hurting people hurt people, and broken-heartedness has a way of clouding up our sight. They did the very best they could to keep us from hurting, but they were aching themselves, and humans can only bear so much, so our parents, being human, hurt us too.

It does something to a child to have two sock drawers and two beds. In this case, less really is more, because just as the monsters under one bed have been silenced and you're finally feeling safe and at-home, you have to leave, abandoning that safe bed for seven long days. And when you come back the next Sunday, there's a fine layer of dust on the cold, unfamiliar sheets, and you know the monsters have moved right back in.

Even if you got to sleep in one bed most of your childhood, I think it's safe to say that we've all got baggage from when we were kids: Maybe your brother always made you feel stupid and left out? Maybe you had to bear witness to your parents cold, loveless marriage, leaving you sad and confused about what love even was? Did your mom try to control your every breath, leaving you unsure of how to speak for yourself as an adult? Did your grandma tell you your legs were too long, your hips too wide? Did fear (or fearful parents/authority figures) convince you to give up on your dreams? Did someone tell you your size was too big or too little? Did someone use your body as if it was their property to do what they'd like with?

That thing that happened to you as a child; that rejection; that pain you felt and still feel? God hates it even more than you do. And if God hates it more than you do, well, you are most certainly allowed to hate it.

I've been working with a trauma therapist for quite some time now, and one of the most valuable things she's shown me is that so much of the pain I feel as an adult is remnants of the fragmented pieces of the little girl inside of me. I know, I know, it sounds hippy-dippy-funky-town at first, but just stick with me for a second. When things happened to us as kids, our brains recorded it in real-time. Of course, what else could happen? The brain can only take in what it's given. The problem is that if we don't at some point go inside ourselves and process that recording, effectively hitting the biological "stop" button, then the recording will just keep playing, skipping over and over like a broken record, leaving that memory in an unprocessed twilight zone and essentially making us continue reliving it as if it were still current reality (this is a big part of why people have PTSD and can suffer intense relapses when in similar "trigger" situations, like when war veterans instantly start ducking under tables and shaking when a car backfires in their suburban neighborhood, thousands of miles away from the battlefield that they suffered trauma in.)

In other words, the reason that for so many years, certain smells would make me sick to my stomach or even trigger flashbacks, was also the reason that spending the night anywhere but my own bed, even well into adulthood, would still give me anxiety: somewhere in my subconscious, the real-time recording of nighttime childhood memories, full of the fear and anxiety that came with constantly switching houses, was triggered to start playing.

# 22
# Pieces

*God already hates me.* The words ping-ponged around my mind as a tear rolled down my cheek. I turned my face away and quickly wiped it off before it reached my lip.

*God already hates me,* I thought again as my heart hammered loudly in my chest. These words covered me, like a wet blanket thrown over a cold child, as I waited for time to pass and for it to end. If it was true—if God already hated me—than what I was doing, or rather, what was being done to me, didn't matter. I had nothing left to lose.

"God already hates me," I thought again, only this time, without meaning to, I whispered the words aloud, soft enough that to me it was the sound of solace covering the skin I wished was hidden, and to him it was just the sound of a soft draft that circled above our heads.

We got dressed in opposite corners of the room, facing away from one another as if we'd met just moments before. My clothes were finally back on, but in every other way I still felt completely naked. Exposed. I wasn't even sure what was left in me to be exposed, but whatever it was, whatever I saw in myself, I hated it and wanted it hidden.

He offered me something to eat, but my stomach was too shaky to feel hungry. His roommates laughed in the corner as they snorted a line of something white; I wasn't sure what. He didn't ask me to leave, but I packed up my things anyway, assuming he wanted me gone now that he'd gotten what he wanted. He offered to walk me to my car, and part of me wondered if, buried somewhere beneath the roughest skin that had ever touched mine, there was a gentleman after all. It seemed like his words *wanted* to be gentle, but his hands showed no interest in it. Maybe he was just as confused as I was: not sure why he did the things he did. I declined his offer, and walked slowly to my car alone.

This had been happening for weeks.

He'd chased me down relentlessly for months leading up to it. I was the only girl that had ever turned him down; not because I was anything special, but because I knew his reputation and was scared of it. But like a skilled predator, he insisted, lurking patiently until he finally caught me one night, vulnerable, weak, and with my guard down.

I was heartbroken after my boyfriend of two years, my first love, had been seen at a party, in the corner of a room, completely wrapped up in some other girl's body. It didn't help that my parents were dealing with their own relational pain, so that whether I was home or not, no one really noticed. So I went to a party with all the coping skills a confused teenager can manage. Out of spite. Out of pain. And Vince was there, prowling, prowling, until he finally pounced.

All I know is I woke up to him, heavy on top of me. Breaking me. He was slow to respond, and slow to move when I tried to push him off. But on the second or third push he finally gave way, rolled over, held his head in his hands for a moment, and then got up and disappeared into a hallway thick with voices.

Everything was spinning and moving slowly all at once. I couldn't breathe or speak. I couldn't move. *What happened? Why am I in this room?* My legs felt completely paralyzed. I rolled over and pressed myself onto the wall the bed was pushed against. I stared directly into the wall, my nose pressed tightly against its cold surface, arms crossed over chest, squinting my eyes hard, open and shut repeatedly. *God, I'm so sorry. I'm so sorry.* I remember whispering half-formulated apologies, praying it was a nightmare and that I would wake up any second. But I didn't wake up. Instead I suffered through the longest, coldest, most frightening night, not fully awake or asleep, pressed tightly against that wall, not wanting to look behind me, just praying that when the sun finally rose, I might too.

When morning came, Vince tried to make conversation. He chuckled innocently beneath his breath, "What happened last night?"

I shrugged my shoulders in his direction, keeping my eyes as far from his as I could, still struggling to catch my breath or to say anything at all. As I stood up, my knees felt brittle, like there was no way I'd make it to my car without every part of me shattering into a million pieces.

I kept my eyes glued ahead and, one careful step at a time, made it to my car. I started the ignition and sat quietly behind the steering wheel for a few long breaths. I tried to listen for the air coming and going through my mouth, to feel some sign of life, to feel anything besides the thousand pounds of shame that shrunk my shoulders in toward my chest and left me feeling hollow.

I finally started driving away, but as I drove I felt a piece of me stay behind, still pressed against that wall, frozen in fear.

I wondered if I'd ever feel whole again.

That piece of me that ached for wholeness grew from a quiet nudge to a loud, muffled shout. So desperate for repair, it drove me back to that same room, that same wall, that same man, again a few weeks later. The very thing that broke me became the thing I couldn't escape. And I went back to him again, and again, and again. That shouting layer of my soul hoped that somehow, in facing what had robbed me, I might find the pieces that were stolen.

I would come home each time after seeing him and lay on the bathtub floor with the showerhead on, wishing the water would wash away the filth I couldn't seem to rub off of my skin. I was thankful for how the water dissolved the tears that often slipped down the drain.

The parties became normal. Regular. What was at first something I went to once out of spite and pain became something I went to regularly as a part of the crowd.

Until one day, when everything changed.

I gave my parents the usual spiel, a bucket full of lies, one layered on top of the next until they became tangled up and hard to keep straight. It was only a matter of time before I got caught.

I came home one night and my dad sat down next to me. "I know that you weren't at Katie's tonight," he said with the gentlest tone—the kind of gentle, defeated tone that only a crushed spirit can muster up. "I drove by her house and didn't see your car. But then I drove by Vince's house...and saw your car there."

My heart dropped into my stomach and all the blood rushed from my face into my fingers as they started to shake. I knew even my dad knew of Vince's reputation. I grabbed a pillow and pulled it into my chest so he couldn't see the trembling.

*This is when I die*, I thought. *My dad is going to kill me.*

He moved closer to me and whispered, "I don't want you to ever feel like you have to lie to me." And then he did the most unimaginable thing. He hugged me, and walked away.

A hug? I would have preferred he kill me. He wasn't mad. He was just so, so sad. Hurt that his daughter lied to him. Hurt that our unique father-daughter bond of trust and honesty had slipped between our fingers. But *most of all,* he was heartbroken that whatever I was doing was something I felt too ashamed to tell him, which could only mean it was hurting me, too.

I crawled into bed and stared at the sky out my window, looking for the stars I could see most nights, but that night, they were nowhere.

The next morning, annoyed that I'd woken up at all and wishing I could hit snooze on my entire adolescence, I turned and saw a piece of paper on my nightstand.

It was a letter. I knew right away that it was written by my dad. I could spot his hardly-legible chicken scratch from a mile away, and no one called me "Lulu" but him:

*Lulu,*

*I just want you to know how special I think you are. You have so many beautiful, amazing gifts to offer the world. And you deserve to be treated with love, kindness, and respect.*

*There's nothing you could ever do that would make me stop loving you. Nothing. No lies or mistakes could ever make me love you less.*

*I'll always love you.*

*No matter what.*

*- Daddy*

That morning I held that letter against my heart and cried.

And cried.

And cried some more. It wasn't a perfect consequence for my actions or a how-dare-you-lie-to-me lecture that changed my life—it was my dad's gentle grace that wrecked me into redemption.

I deserved to be grounded until kingdom come for lying night after night, for drinking underage, for dabbling in drugs, for going back to Vince, for choosing poison over and over again. But where I deserved to be handed a punishment, my dad chose to hand me a love letter.

And I still can't write that out without crying both of my eyeballs entirely out of their sockets.

So, Dad, thank you. That letter, written with so much love and gentleness, changed my life. On some level though, I hope that you never read this chapter. I can't imagine a father's pain reading in uncomfortable graphic detail the things that his daughter experienced, things out of his control. So if you do, thank you for having the courage to read this, and more importantly, thank you for having the courage to choose grace.

I decided that morning that I couldn't go on living this way. I couldn't keep drowning myself and the people I loved in lies. It wasn't a perfect overnight success story. But I started taking steps; steps away from the parties, the friends, and from Vince. It got harder before it got better, though. When you have friends who center their lives on parties, sex and alcohol, and you stop wanting to go to parties, have sex, and drink alcohol, all of a sudden you become the outsider, the weird girl, the prude.

I was isolated. Depressed. Confused. Searching for the pieces of me that had been shattered. In fact, I'm still not entirely sure how I graduated high school since I skipped almost every one of my classes my senior year.

But, there's just something about hitting rock bottom, isn't there? All the normal garbage you go to for fulfillment just doesn't cut it anymore.

I may have been isolated, but with the isolation came a stillness. A stillness I needed. It gave me space to wrestle with my spirit—I didn't know what I was doing or what I believed, but I started reading "Start your day Right", a biblical daily devotional read by Joyce Meyer. (I figured the baby step of "starting my day right" would be a move in the right direction at least, even if I had no idea what any of it meant.) The devotionals were only about three sentences long per day, which was about all I could handle at the time.

But those three sentences a day were enough to slowly replace the only sentence I'd been believing about God for almost two years: that He hated me. The things I read sounded a lot like the letter I read that morning from my dad. God, I came to find out, didn't hate me.

Not only did He not hate me, He loved me wildly.

## 23
# A Breather

I never want to assume that you believe in God, or even that you're comfortable hearing from someone who does. I hope by now you've gotten to know me enough to feel how important it is to me that I don't shove my beliefs down your throat. The only reason I share this with you is on the off-chance that you walk around carrying some shame from your past just like I did.

If we were sitting across from each other at a coffee shop right now, I would grab your hand and *only* tell you what I'm about to tell you because finding it out, for me, lifted a weight off of my shoulders that had been crushing me. If there is even the slightest chance that it might lift weight off of you too, I can't *not* tell you.

I really truly believe that when the Creator of the Universe looks at *you,* the first things He sees isn't what you've done or what's been done to you. It's love. Just overwhelming, heart-pounding-out-of-your-chest *love*. It's a smile that stretches from one side of the planet to the other, when God looks at you, and I don't know if you've taken a stroll around the planet recently, but that is really freaking wide.

Whatever is in your past—heck, whatever happened

earlier *today*—He saw it *all*, and still chooses you. He still loves you. He still wants you. He still fights for you.

The beauty of this Creator of the Universe, the God I put my faith in (even if some days, it's a teeny tiny wobbly faith), is that we're allowed to say no to that love-invite. Because real love is free, not forced.

I said no for a really long time. But when I finally said yes, everything started to change.

## 24
# Bruised

I was working at my first official adult job at a pediatric office. My mom and I got lunch together every other week or so, and our relationship was on the mend and we were building trust again. We were driving to our favorite sandwich shop a few minutes from my office when I thought I noticed some strange marks on her neck as I glanced at her from the passenger seat. At first, I felt uncomfortable because I thought they were hickies she was trying to cover up with makeup. Her new partner had recently moved in, and we were all still trying to decide if we felt good about the move because we weren't sure if they were good for each other. I almost didn't say anything because I felt embarrassed, but the words spit out of me without warning and I teasingly said, "Whatchya got on your neck there, Mooooom?" It was a bold move for me; I wasn't used to being that transparent or even playful with her.

Now I know God probably pushed the words out of my mouth to give her a window to say something.

She got really quiet and avoided my eyes. After a few uncomfortably long seconds, she told me that the hickies were not hickies at all. They were bruises. her partner had choked her during an argument just a couple days prior.

Finding out news like that about someone you love... it's so many things crashing together in one instant. It felt like electricity shot through my veins. I wanted to punch a wall. Scream. Cry. Call the police. Freak OUT. But instead, I froze. I think feeling all of those things at once put me in a state of shock that allowed me to just be silent, to just sit with my mom with zero judgement, and just listen. I think it's what she needed most at the time. She told me her partner was going to start going to anger management. I was suspicious about that and nervous about her staying at the house. And with good reason.

A few weeks later my mom showed up at our apartment to talk to us.

She sat down on our living room floor and proceeded to tell us that my very worst nightmare almost came true.

She had noticed earlier that there was a gun case tucked away under the bed that she had never seen before. She got scared and hid the gun so that her partner couldn't find it, because she didn't know what the motives were for having it. A few days later, they got into an argument, which escalated into a full-on physical altercation. As they each went to separate parts of the house after fighting, my mom heard her partner scream down the stairs, "Where is it?!" (my mom's gut reaction in knowing that a person with these types of extreme anger issues should never own a gun may have saved her life that day.) When she didn't answer, her partner ran downstairs and said, "I don't need a gun," then proceeded to grab a kitchen knife. Thank GOD there happened to be some family staying in the house who happened to arrive just in time to break up the fight. Aside from some bruising, my mom was physically unharmed, but the emotional damage, as you can imagine, would weigh on her and on the rest of us for much, much longer.

That night could have ended so much worse. A restraining order was filed, and my mom came to stay with us for a few days.

Here's the thing though: my mom had been on the board of the Cocoon Shelter, a local safe house for victims of domestic violence. She knew all the warning signs of physical abuse and had even taught seminars to empower women to stand up and get help. She had even started a company whose sole mission was to give victims of domestic violence a job so that they could leave their abusers and get on their feet. And yet, with all of that knowledge and experience, years later she found herself in the same predicament as so many of the women she had helped in the past. All it takes is crossing paths with a manipulative person who slowly breaks down your boundaries and desensitizes you toward their twisted way of showing love.

And even though it happened to someone I love and not me directly, I knew it was important to mention in a book that talks about all the ways we are shut down, made small or insignificant, because I can't think of anything that shuts down the human heart more than having someone who says they love you with their mouth then use that same mouth to verbally abuse you, and with the same hands that had shown you love, strike you.

It was one of the most terrifying times of my life. I felt like I was going to puke from anxiety any second that I wasn't with my mom for those first few weeks after it happened. I texted her every five minutes to make sure she was safe. As important as this topic is though, I struggled to include it in this book, because it doesn't feel like my story to tell. So, I asked my mom to share, with her own words, what she would want to say if she was sitting across from a woman who is either currently stuck in an abusive relationship, or playing re-runs in her mind from a past abusive relationship. If you are reading this and that is you or someone you love, I hope my mom's simple words speak to your soul.

"If you don't feel loved; really, truly loved for *who you are*, get out. Look for tender, real love. Look for someone who's actions you don't have to make excuses for. But mostly, get to know you and learn to love yourself just as you are. Believe with every fiber of your being that the person looking back at you in the mirror deserves to be loved and treated like a queen, and settle for nothing less."

## 25
# Breaking the Loop

The other reason I knew I needed to include my mom's story in here is that it's important to note the generational effects of re-runs when we allow them to keep looping.

My great-grandfather was a famous opera singer in Spain (I know, right?! Kind of epic!), but because he lived a life on the road, his son, my grandfather, lived year-round in a boarding school. And yes, I mean a boarding school like the stereotypical ones you see in the movies—every time my family watches the play *Scrooge* and we see him as a child left alone watching all the other kids get picked up by their parents for the holidays, my mom gets really sad because she says that's what it was like for my grandpa.

As I've already mentioned a million times, hurting people hurt people, and whatever unresolved pain from his young life that my grandpa had, he carried into his adulthood and into his fatherhood. It's so hard to know how to love your child well when the only example of love you saw was distorted, and so although my grandpa was present for his kids—something he never got to experience—he also had a temper.

If you meet him now, you'd never imagine it. Now, he's always wanting to bring joy wherever he is. He cracks the same jokes over and over again and I never get tired of them. He is gentle and sweet and even nurturing. After my grandmother walked through a house-fire to save her infant child (another crazy epic story for another time), he would gently put ointment on her feet every single night, and to this day he still puts lotion on her feet every night before bed.

You would never believe that he hit his children. You would never believe that my mom, being the oldest, often took the blame for things her siblings did, so that she would get the punishment instead of them, and oh man did she get it.

But you'd also never believe that my grandfather was doing the very best he could. And once he realized that his very best was absolutely destroying his family, he did better. He stood up in front of his entire church congregation and confessed his mistakes to his family and asked for their forgiveness (and if you know anything about Cubans in Miami at Catholic mass, you know that the church was most likely packed to standing room only. Pardon my French, but that took some serious balls.)

The thing is, we both attract and are attracted to the kind of love that we understand. It's the reason so many dads take their daughters out on dates—they want them to understand what it's like to be treated with love and respect on a date. They want their daughters' standards to be high. I am sure that my grandfather wanted those same standards for my mom, but unfortunately, my mom found herself in a marriage with someone who also had a temper. My dad was never physically abusive with her or with any of us, and he too has since become a much more peace-filled man, but at the start of their marriage, his anger resembled that same anger my mom saw in her dad. Even after my mom and dad divorced, my mom continually found herself in different kinds of abusive relationships, whether it was emotional abuse, infidelity, addiction, or domestic violence. I watched my mom battle through these kinds of relationships, and since I didn't really have a healthy relationship modeled, I too was uncertain about what love ought to be, and so I too had my fair share of differing levels and kinds of abuse (or at the very least, not being treated the way I deserved.)

All of these stories repeated throughout generations, where the characters change but the plot stays the same, are re-runs. Someone has to break the chain. If I would have married any of the men I dated before my husband, my daughter would have most likely grown up seeing her mom being treated like garbage. Before my husband, I had never dated anyone who didn't cheat on me. I had never dated anyone that respected and honored my body. I had never dated anyone who truly, unconditionally, loved me.

I remember that when my husband and I first started dating and I noticed him being what I thought was "overly" kind, it almost annoyed me or seemed unattractive to me. I was used to being treated like trash. I was used to being attracted to a different kind of man, the kind of man who wouldn't really commit to me, who left me hanging, who flirted with other women while I was in the same room. In other words, I was used to dating boys.

Thankfully, I married Ricky, and now my daughter gets to see what it's like to date an honorable man, full of integrity, both gentle and full of strength. She gets to have that as her standard, because I finally did the dirty work of finding out what re-runs had been playing on loop not only in my mind, but in the minds of multiple generations of my family.

# 26
# Why You Push My Boy

My grandparents fled Cuba just as things were getting bad with Fidel Castro. They went to Venezuela to seek refuge, and then wanted to move from Venezuela to Miami, but as they were getting ready for that final move, there was one teeny-weeny-itsy-bitsy complication—my grandma was eight months pregnant with their first child; way past the limit of pregnancy that you were allowed to get on a plane with. But they were absolutely determined to find a way. They wanted their first child to be born in the States so that he or she wouldn't struggle like they had and could just be born an American citizen without any of the complications that come with being an immigrant. But my grandmother was just too pregnant to fly...so they told a little white lie on the doctor's paperwork and said that she was MUCH less further along than she actually was. It was a little white lie that could have turned into a very big mess had she literally gone into labor at 35,000 feet, but it was a risk they were willing to take.

They arrived in Miami on November 23, 1963, and 15 days later, my mom was born. They were still living in a hotel for crying out loud! I can't even imagine traveling with only the clothes on my back and having a baby 15 days later while living in a hotel. When my daughter was born, I had my own warm comfy bed, Netflix to binge on during all the weird leaky hours of the night spent nursing, a Boppy, a Tula baby carrier, 75 different kinds of swaddle blankets, a month of free meals from a church meal train, and gluten-free donuts every morning and a hormone balancing green smoothie every night courtesy of my amazing husband. My grandma had a smelly hotel room, a language she didn't speak, and most likely, cans of beans to recover. But their daughter was an American citizen; the very first generation in our family to be a U.S. citizen, and that made it all worth it.

I think every generation has re-runs they are trying to break away from. It's the reason there's so much grace in parenting. We spend so much time recovering from our own childhood, and then when we're thrown blindly into our own parenting, all we can think of is what we'll do differently than our parents. Along the way, we do things that we don't realize will hurt our kids; stuff they'll spend time healing from and then avoid doing with their own kids. Having re-runs to wrestle through doesn't make us wrong, shameful, or messed up—it makes us human.

* * *

My grandmother's English was broken and she rarely used it, but obviously she would do pretty much anything to protect her babies, like most of us mamas would. One day she went to pick up her kids from school and saw my uncle, her first son, being picked on and pushed down by another kid. All her beautiful Cuban fire exploded out of the car in a flash and she ran toward that bully screaming at him, "*Why you push my boy?!*" Those words are now legend in my family. We say them often. We revel in the fact that my grandma, the matriarch, the strong silent type, didn't skip a beat to speak out, to protect, to defend.

The thing about re-runs is that we're allowed to simultaneously love and honor the people who gave us scars, while not tolerating the wounds that replay in our minds because of them. We are allowed to look at those loops and say, "*Why you push my boy?!*" in defense of our own souls. And as we defend ourselves, we're defending the generations of souls that will come after us. Re-runs are bullies. They will continue invading our space, thoughts, and minds and will push us around until we finally point a finger directly at them, call them out, and remove our eight year-old self from that divorce, or our 15 year-old self from that rape, or our 19 year-old self from that PTSD, and we can hug those versions of ourselves and assure them that they are safe now; they don't have to keep sprinting around in circles to avoid the danger. They can rest now. And as they rest, so do we.

**Strip Off: Re-runs**

The undealt-with trauma from our past keeps us small because it keeps pieces of us in prisons. My past doesn't define me and I don't have to fear it. Getting it all out on the table doesn't make me a failure, it makes me free.

**Step Into: The Freedom of Letting Go**

Today, what if we pick something out of our closet that we keep out of obligation, insecurity, or just because it's in the dark, scary corner of the closet that we don't feel like dealing with, and got rid of it? It can be a baby step toward letting go of old ways of thinking, belief systems, or re-runs on loop in our mind. Step into the freedom that comes with letting go of excess baggage.

**GV Fashion Tip**

The same one shirt can be worn so many different ways. Don't stick to all the familiar ways you wear what you already own, see if you can take something old (like a re-run in our minds) and turn it into something fresh, redeemed, and lovely. Try slouching a shoulder, pulling the sleeves up halfway, tying a knot, buttoning it all the way up one day then halfway down the next with a cute undershirt. Layering is magic. Redeeming old things to be lovely and new-on-you is spiritual fashion, girl.

*You can take an out-of-date piece and spruce it up with your own style—it's the reason style is forever, even if fashion is fleeting.*

# LONEWOLF LIVING

# 27
# Sweatpants and Manicures

We've moved precisely eleven times in our short seven years of marriage. (I know, I know. It's a lot of moving.) Thankfully, only two of those moves were cross-country and the rest were to neighboring cities for different jobs.

With all the moving we've had the chance to be a part of many different communities, most of which, we were introduced to through going to church. While there were lots of unique aspects about each church we went to, for the most part, they've all had a similar structure when it comes to building community (something we longed for deeply). On Sunday mornings, we'd gather to sing songs, pray, listen to one of the leaders speak, sing some more songs, run into people on the walk to the car (or the sprint if you're chasing a toddler like I am these days), and then we'd go home. We'd also have "groups" during the week outside of Sunday gatherings. Most American Christian churches have them, and they go by any number of names: Life Groups, Small Groups, Focus Groups, Home Groups...you get the point. All the groups! It was sweet to have a regular rhythm with people.

I love and appreciate the mission of these types of groups. How can you gather a group of people consistently and intentionally without calling it a thing or having some sort of structure or plan? How can new people meet their church family (if that's what they're looking for) if you don't have a place and time for them to find you at? It's so important.

But some days—the days when I'm most honest with myself—my spirit craves for more than just structured events or a weekly routines. Some days it's not routine events I long for in my friendships, but real, raw, come-over-even-when-I-don't-have-real-pants-on-and-my-house-is-a-mess friendships.

I definitely don't have all the answers, but I think there might be some organic, authentic options, in addition to what we already do (not instead of, because really, these groups are equally important, too). There has to be. Because so many of us are really lonely. We are lonely even when we are with each other. We are sad and isolated even when we are smack dab in the middle of "community".

As I was thinking about this, I came across Dr. Andrew Solomon, a brilliant psychology professor who traveled the world studying depression and anxiety in different communities. On one of his trips, Solomon spent time in Cambodia interviewing survivors of the civil war that broke out during the dictatorship of Pol Pot (known as the Khmer Rouge) where more than 20% of the population was slaughtered.

Just days before he left, Solomon met with a woman named Phaly Nuon, whose personal survival story was absolutely horrifying. However, Phaly used her suffering to help save others. She was nominated for a Nobel Peace Prize for the incredible work she is doing. Phaly sett up an orphanage and center for depressed women in Phnom Penh, or as Solomon describes it, "she's achieved astonishing success in resuscitating women whose mental afflictions are such that other doctors have left them for dead" (36).

Her recovery center had a three step approach and it drew me in—I'd never heard of anything like it. She believed that the keys to bringing severely traumatized women back to life are to 1) Forget the trauma, 2) Learn to work, and 3) Learn to love.

The forgetting portion included things like meditation, distraction, and unofficial talk therapy, where all Phaly did was sit with the women for hours until they finally were able to tell their story. She just listened. She let them learn to use their voice, share their story, build trust, and be vulnerable with at least one person. I'm not sure if they could ever actually forget the trauma they experienced, but when you bring trauma into the light, it loses some of its power.

The second portion, teaching them to work, was also crucial. Phaly explained that, "They must learn to do these things well and have pride in them." I hear "work" and I think "purpose" or "mission," which I believe can breathe life into anyone's bones. The women began working on all sorts of different things; some volunteering at the camp, some making art, and so on. Sometimes a lack of purpose is enough to spiral a person into depression or isolation. She helped them find purpose again.

Lastly, Phaly focused on helping women learn to love. This is the one that flipped a switch in me as I read it. How could anyone teach a person so broken from horror, so traumatized, so stunted and even pronounced "dead" by some doctors, how to love? I figured the approach she took on this one would be complicated. Profound. Deep. But It wasn't. It was shockingly simple.

Her brilliantly simple strategy? First help them feel clean with a bath. Then teach them how to give one another manicures and pedicures—how to take care of their fingernails, because doing so made them feel beautiful, "and they want so much to feel beautiful," she explains. Not only did it help them feel beautiful, but most importantly, it put them in contact with the bodies of other people and made them give up their bodies to the care of others. It rescued them from physical isolation, which was all they knew, and that led to the breakdown of their emotional isolation.

While they were together, washing, doing their nails, sitting, and just existing, they started talking to each other. And slowly over time, they learned to trust one another. By the end, they had learned how to make friends "so that they will never have to be so lonely and so alone again". And even their stories, which up until then they had told to no one except Phaly Nuon, started being shared with one another.

"Grooming," says Nuon, "is one of the primary forms of socialization among primates, and this return to grooming as a socializing force among human beings struck me as curiously organic." Maybe the words primates and grooming freak you out. I am not saying we are monkeys. But I am saying that sometimes, I overcomplicate things. Sometimes, what I need is simpler than I think. When I think I feel the urge to call the doctor, move to a new city, or sign up for the next exercise class at the Y, I might actually just need to take a nap, go on a walk, get some fresh air, or sit in the presence of another human with zero agenda and zero makeup on. I might just need some primal needs met, like air, sleep, human connection.

What if sometimes we need to get together and wear sweatpants instead of our Sunday best, and bring nail polish and hair brushes instead of Bibles studies and agendas?

There is a time and place for all of it, of course. I think studying Scripture (or whatever you study for spiritual and personal connection and growth) is absolutely necessary and important in relationships. But sometimes, sisters, we need to just sit together for long enough, just doing each others' nails (or doing whatever), that eventually, our stories spill out, raw, unrushed and unscheduled.

After the three-step healing process, the women from the camp in Thailand became an incredible community that does life together daily and takes care of orphans together. Three simple steps: forget, work, love. How often do we overcomplicate it, left with our loneliness and convinced that we are the problem? That we are unloved and unwanted? And how simple could it be to finally find a way out of that lonely mindset?

When I overcomplicate things, I feel left out—sometimes, I'm even convinced I've forgotten how to make friends all together. It's embarrassing to admit, especially when being a part of such missional churches over the years, because sometimes it can feel like if we aren't serving a greater purpose or doing something 'spiritual', then our time together is not significant. But I think it's actually the mundane, everyday things (i.e., sitting in sweats and painting each other's nails) done together that can strengthen us spiritually, because sitting with someone in both silence and chatter as we "groom" is spiritual. It is significant, because it's vulnerable. It's organic, and we all know organic everything is all the rage right now—we just forget that the most important organic thing we need in life is relationships.

The problem, of course, is that just like those dang organic berries cost double the price of regular berries, organic, true friendship without an agenda actually comes with a higher price tag...because it's scary. Heck, it can be downright petrifying! You mean I have to be real, and take off my makeup and let my guard down and possibly face judgment?! But ladies, we can do it! We are innately wired for it, actually. Before any of us ever experienced rejection for the first time, we were so much better at it—we didn't walk up to kids on the playground and say, "Do you want to come to this weekly Barbie convention group thing? There'll be people you know there! And you'll get free snacks!" No, instead we just looked them unashamedly in the eyes across the teeter totter and asked, "Will you be my friend?" (Talk about being vulnerable! How terrifying would that be now?)

So I've been approaching friendship differently these days. I'm not rushing to sign up for every bible study group under the sun, and I'm not even feeling guilty if I don't attend every structured event. But I am inviting women over to share space with me, often with a text that goes something like this: "Want to sit around in sweatpants together?" And my friendships are changing. They are so real, you guys. I just don't have the time or energy anymore to wear masks. So we ditch our masks, and we find stuff we love to do together: play music, paint nails, watch movies, go to a hip-hop dance class; whatever. And you know what? Deep conversation happens naturally. Silent moments happen naturally. Laughter happens naturally.

Those agenda-less moments approached without a need to fill every minute with a discussion prompt are the moments that make us family. And we need family—humans that know us deeply—just as much as we need water.

So let's stop rushing the process or jumping ahead to conquer the moment before we're even hydrated enough to walk. Hydrate first, conquer second. In other words: once we've shared unrushed time and listened to each other's stories, dreams, and painted our nails, then we can go change the world together.

## 28
# My Boyfriend Will Probably Fall in Love With Her

I traveled to Mumbai, India with a small group of college friends for a ten-day mission trip my junior year of college. The trip was primarily made up of women—young girls like myself wanting to step outside ourselves and our small-town school to serve the world, feed the hungry, free the enslaved, and spread the Good News of the Gospel to the ends of the earth (*I know, I know*...I was so holy; a regular ole modern-day Mother Teresa,) and we got to spend the trip sharing food and love with the homeless and meeting and helping women stuck in India's overwhelming sex-trafficking epidemic.

And while I felt quite blessed and Mother Teresa-y to be there, what I didn't mention to anyone was that I also went because first of all, my boyfriend was going, and second of all, I was terrified that if I *didn't* go, said boyfriend would fall in love with one of the other girls on the trip. (This may make more sense when you read about my addictions in the next section, but for now we'll just say it was rooted in debilitating fears, insecurities, and paranoia.)

Turns out, though, I wasn't the only one there with insecurities and debilitating fears. Yep—when you have a group of women together in a situation where there is a bigger mission at hand and where the talents and beauty and gifts of those women are needed to accomplish something for the greater good, you inevitably have immense temptation for competition and comparison.

These beautiful, gifted women can so easily find themselves stuck in their own heads, questioning, *am I making a difference? Do I have anything good to offer? Am I beautiful amidst all of this beauty, or am I just white noise next to all of these other women? (Oh, and is my boyfriend falling madly in love with that other girl as she offers the snacks in her purse to the starving child on the street?)*

Add to all of the above the fact that we were all in a third-world country where we were completely out of our comfort zones and couldn't so much as speak enough of the native tongue to ask where the nearest bathroom was, and insecurities spread like wildfire.

But about three days in to the ten-day trip, we had a powerful night around a fire confessing our comparison. A handful of us spoke about feeling insecure in ourselves and our value, and then confessed to crossing the line from admiration to jealousy of each other. One girl in particular (who I thought was just-so-beautiful and who I was *convinced* my man would fall in love with) had apparently been feeling the same way toward me. She saw my beauty and felt insecure in her own. And I saw her beauty and felt inadequate in mine. We sat together, in shock that we were both feeling the exact same things about each other.

But as we gave voice to our fears and brought them into the light, the most amazing thing happened: I felt the weight lifting, and I could see it lift from her, too.

I remember the window ledge that we sat on as we talked. We had never really had a conversation before that trip, even though we'd been going to the same school and involved in the same ministry organization for a few years already. Who knew that flying across the world would be the catalyst that would bring our souls together in mutual understanding and vulnerability?

What's really incredible is that six years later, that *same girl* who sat across from me on the window ledge that day in Mumbai would be the woman who assisted at the birth of my daughter and actually *caught* my sweet baby girl. And then just a few months later, I assisted at the birth of *her* daughter. Those walls torn down years before on our mission trip allowed us to join hands to love the people in Mumbai well, 'birthing' life in small ways like feeding starving children or giving hope to enslaved women, and then literally helping each other give birth years later.

Ladies.

If we are willing to lay down our comparison and begin celebrating each other, the amount of life that will be born and depression that will die is *too huge for me to even find words for.*

...Ahem, but I'm gonna try anyway.

Unimaginable.

Inconceivable.

Marvelously Freeing.

MELT-YOUR-FACE-OFF BEAUTIFUL.

Epic.

Freefunktastic.

Yeah, that's a word now. Because I don't think we've really done this well yet. I think we are just starting to scratch the surface but have yet to truly grasp the LIFE that is possible when we take each other by the hand DAILY, not just at retreats or baby showers when we're in a little safe friend-bubble or on a spiritual mountaintop away from the real world. And I think we're unaware of the DEATH that happens when we don't reach out to one another in vulnerability daily.

In light of all of these glorious revelations about my struggles with comparison and competition, I have made a habit of proactively battling comparison with celebration. If you hop on my Facebook page you will see share after share of the things that the women in my life are doing beautifully. I celebrate the crap out of my friends. Sometimes I wonder if people ever avoid my page because it's almost spam with how many posts I have shared about other women acting courageously and being beautiful. I share the blogs that they write, the videos they make, the events they are planning, the spaces they design, the talks they give, the art they paint. I share it all. I'm a serial sharer and a serial celebrator. And I feel perfectly fine with that.

I share beauty when I'm inspired because there was a time when the beauty in others would have caused me to compete or compare, even if it was just on a deeply subconscious level. So it's an active daily discipline to celebrate and share that beauty with others. And you know what? I can genuinely say that I can't even remember the last time I felt comparison or jealousy. But that's because I am proactively 'killing the sin before it kills me'.

Let's celebrate the beauty around us as a preventative *routine* instead of a *reaction* to comparison.

I think it's just as serious and slippery of a slope as any other addiction someone might struggle with. This may be overstating my case, but I believe that those who haven't given in to their addictions in a long time are able to keep staying strong because they take proactive steps to battle it *daily*. If it's a porn addiction, they may have software on their computers to hold them accountable, or an accountability partner who regularly checks in and challenges them to keep their eyes on what's good and honorable. If it's alcoholism, they may go to AA multiple times a week. And queens, we need to encourage and challenge each other similarly to daily keep our eyes on what's good and honorable. I won't let you compare yourself to me or to anyone else, because you have too much beauty to offer to think that another's beauty diminishes yours.

If our default is to compete, then we will *by default* be anxious and depressed. The competitive mind is an exhausted soul and a bogged-down, tense body; it's heavy to carry, and not only does life feel like a perpetual race to sprint through or mountain to climb, but we also miss out on our real purpose and on the gifts we uniquely bring to the table because we are too busy looking at the gifts someone else brings and wondering how we match up.

## 29
# Climbing Mountains

My husband Ricky and I lived in Colorado for one short summer. We spent most of our time visiting breweries, taking seminary classes, and climbing mountains with friends (#dream, right?)

If you've ever climbed a mountain before, you know that this interesting thing happens as you get higher and higher—the air pressure changes and it becomes harder to breathe.

I think life is sometimes like climbing a mountain. We try new things, we learn new things, we take risks, we decide to move up toward something—a goal, a dream, a new job, whatever—and it's scary, and can sometimes take our breath away, but it's always totally worth it.

But when we get competitive, we also start racing. Can you imagine trying to climb a mountain and instead of taking your time, checking your footing, and steadying your breath as the altitude changes, you're constantly looking through your peripherals to make sure no one is passing you by? It seems so dangerous. I am not coordinated enough to rush climbing a mountain; I would slip and trip and face-plant into the dirt and then roll off the nearest ledge.

Whatever mountains we're climbing, dreams we're chasing, or visions we're pursuing, we just can't hike alone or race others to the top. When I believe the top of the mountain is a race to win instead of a view to share, I am anxious, depressed, lonely, and isolated. Do you know what it would feel like if you got to the top, looked around, and had no one to share the view with?

It's *so* much more fun when, instead of being so concerned with the women to our left and our right and constantly wondering, *"Are they going to pass me? Am I lapping them?"*, we slow down and look around to the women above and below and alongside us who are also climbing the same mountain. "We're all in this together" is such a cliche (even though, ahem, I have to admit it's still my favorite song from *High School Musical)*, but the reality is that it's also *genuinely* helpful and mutually beneficial to all of us if I am looking up to the woman ahead of me who's reaching back a hand and saying, "Come with me! I want you to see this view!" And then, as I climb up the next ledge with the help of a friend, I can turn around and reach back and offer my strength to help pull someone else up. We were never meant to hike alone, and we were never meant to compete at the expense of others.

30
# Not White Noise

Before I started *celebrating* others daily, I was held *captive* daily. I used to get anxious and even sick to my stomach by how nervous I was that my boyfriend would fall in love with the pretty girl at whichever event we were at, even if the "event" was breakfast at a cafe or standing in line at the DMV. Do you know how emotionally *exhausting* it is to think that at any minute you are going to be betrayed, rejected, or made to feel not enough? It's like running a perpetual marathon while carrying a pregnant elephant on your back. What? You've never done that before? Well trust me, I have, and it is not pretty.

Every boyfriend I had before Ricky had cheated on me, so I had at least *some* reason for being so paranoid, but there came a point where all it was doing was imprisoning me and I could hardly hold a conversation because of how anxious I was, constantly checking my peripherals for the pretty women he could be choosing over me.

One day I finally got so fed up with it that I wrote a blog post in an attempt to punch my comparison and scarcity mindset in the face. I'd had an epiphany that I wanted to write a blog post fully describing how beautiful one of my friends was (ok, if I'm being honest, specifically one of my friends who I was always comparing myself to because she was so drop-dead gorgeous.) With this specific friend, I constantly teetered on the edge between fan-girly admiration and mean-girl jealousy of her beauty and gifts. I always felt concerned my boyfriend would fall in love with her—which was completely unfounded. They had never shown even the tiniest sign of interest in each other, and in fact, she was one of the friends who I admired the most in her marriage and the way she and her husband had healthy boundaries with the opposite sex. It was purely in my head and I wrote a blog post (called "Celebrating Beauty") about all the amazing lovely things that I found in her. The moment I clicked "Post", it was like a weight had lifted, like I had finally stepped outside of the prison that I had been living in. I wrote that blog about ten years ago, and I've been practicing this discipline ever since; not always perfectly of course, but I'm fighting the good fight daily!

Women, we HAVE to cut off competition before it cuts *us* up into so many pieces that we forget how it feels to be whole and secure in who we are, and lose our ability to offer *our* gifts and beauty to others. When we help each other pick up our cut-up pieces—when we celebrate each other instead of compete with one another—we are powerful. We are a force to be reckoned with. Your beauty isn't white noise in a room full of other beautiful women, it's a voice in harmony with others that needs to be heard, seen, and shared. Your gifts aren't runner up next to your talented friend's gifts. There is so much room for each of us at the table, and the more we lift one another up, the more we each stand out in a crowd.

31
# Brilliant Beauty

"Sing. Just...sing."

My dear friend Vanessa, who was a number of years older than me, had every coolness gene you could possibly have. She was beautiful, athletic, hilarious, and ridiculously talented—one of those freaks of nature that the universe seems to have blessed with the ability to do everything. And the girl would bring you to tears when she opened her mouth to sing! I loved singing too, and it would have been so easy to feel less than or insignificant in her presence. But instead, one day she sat down next to me, closed her eyes, and told me to sing. She didn't even sing along with me like I thought she might; she just listened, smiling softly, fully present in the moment and in my voice (which was likely a very shaky scared-little-girl voice.) And then she encouraged my socks off, going into detail in describing what she loved about my voice. She was so at peace with who she was that she didn't even skip a beat in giving me space to sing or in celebrating my gifts, even if they were the same exact gifts she had. Sometimes we're only willing to encourage others if their gifts don't compete with ours. But not Vanessa. And you know what? To this day, she's still one of the people I just wish I could be around more. You know the kind of people who are just such incredible life-givers that everyone craves their presence? That's her. And because of how she encouraged me, I think of her often when I'm encouraging women around me. She was so at peace with how God made her that she didn't always need to be in the limelight and could use her brilliance to shine a light on others.

And you know what? She wasn't alone. I remember realizing that, similar to Vanessa, the people around me who were most at peace in their skin were also the people who stopped comparing themselves with those in their peripherals. These were the women in my life who taught me how to be the kind of beautiful that doesn't fade with age. That's the kind of brilliant beauty I want to be. That's the kind of beauty that makes others crave being around someone. That's the kind of beauty that is steady and unchanging, no matter how many kids you have or boxes of donuts you consume. They were so confident in the way God made them that lifting up *others* came naturally. When I avoid lifting up others, it's out of fear that it'll bring me lower, but when I go out of my way to lift up others, it's because I know my place is untouchable and steady; their rising value doesn't lower my own.

Let's be the kind of beauty that makes space for more beauty.

## 32
# Stand Up Tall and Speak Anyway

Right before I turned hundreds of pages of writing in to my editor, a little voice in the back of my head started nagging me about something I had left out. A little part of me couldn't believe I was about to turn in an entire manuscript about refusing to shrink myself down out of fear...and yet fear had kept me from writing one of the more difficult (but most important) pieces of all of my healing. This is the story of the time I felt myself shrink more than I ever had before (and ever would again.) The most inspiring version of these events would be something along the lines of an epic feminist underdog story where some bully of a man used his strength against me, making me feel insignificant, and me and a band of sisters in lipstick-warpaint rose up to fight his misogynistic tyranny and scored one for womankind. And yes—gender inequalities are totally a thing, don't get me wrong. But in reality, it's not *always* men who make women feel small, is it? So much more often than we'd like to admit, it's us women making each other feel small.

When I was around ten years old, my dad got remarried. For sixteen years, we were the modern-day Brady Bunch: six kids total, three from my dad's previous marriage (my two brothers and me), and three from hers.

Some days, we all got along: we laughed, we danced, we cried, we made memories. But those days became increasingly few and far between as the years passed. Both my dad and step-mom walked in to their marriage carrying enough baggage from their pasts for a trip to the moon. Ah, baggage. It's what makes blended families so hard. You aren't building a life together from a fresh slate, you're being thrown in to a life together with years and years of baggage to sort through from the past (previous marriages most likely) and years and years of being parents already. And in our blended family, because 99% of my dad and step-mom's baggage had gone undealt with AND because each of them expressed their pain in unique and unhealthy ways, codependency became a way of life for us kids. Walking on eggshells was, well, just how we walked. We were always nervous we were going to say the wrong thing, do the wrong thing, or *be* the wrong thing—too happy, too excited, too loud, too quiet, too *anything*. It became an incredible source of anxiety for me, and for sixteen years my soul shriveled up and stayed quiet in order to not rock the boat.

Now, my goal here is not to put anyone on blast. My stepmom had a good heart. She cooked and cleaned tirelessly and ran the household the best she could with six crazy kids (three of which were not her blood). But her specific baggage made it really hard for her to love, or even like me. It does something to a young girl to walk into a home and feel embarrassed to speak, let alone grab something to eat from the fridge because she feels unwanted and unwelcome.

For sixteen years I felt like I had to walk around the house like a quiet little mouse, tip-toeing around, trying not to cause any ruckus. I remember not being allowed to celebrate when I made a sports team in high school, or when I got a scholarship for college. If almost anything good happened at all, our joy of it got stuffed and shrunken down because of the jealousy, comparison, or bitterness our celebration was always met with. I began associating "good news" with shame and sadness, because if something good happened in my life, it gave the people in my house more reason to dislike me. So, I stopped celebrating all together.

To this day, I start shrinking when I am sharing something I'm excited about. I can't tell you how many times I've been talking to my friends about this book and they've lovingly gotten in my face and said, "Don't you dare make this small, Gelly May! Stand up tall, don't shrink!" My excitement and pride in a project is always met with shame and my default is to shrink and make the thing I'm excited about smaller. It has taken time, love, compassion, support, and lots of counseling and prayer for the shame which has been so ingrained in me to begin to rewire, but the important part is that no matter how much it terrifies me, I'm not letting my default position (to get *small* in order to stay *safe*) define my default response: to stand up *tall* and *speak* anyway.

The thing is, I don't think it requires sixteen years in a blended family with lots of baggage for you to know what I'm talking about. Have you ever made yourself small around another woman because you could tell she was competitive or insecure, and you didn't want to make her feel bad about herself, so you lessened who you are so that she might feel better about who she is?

Me, too, sister. Me, too.

This is a delicate line to walk. I love that my empathy and sensitivity allows me to read the room; to feel the energy of a sister next to me and decide how I'd like to respond. I love when I get to lift up a sister who I see struggling with insecurity, because so many times I've had sisters who have gone out of their way to lift me up, help me feel safe, give me a voice when they've seen me shrinking in the back of a room. The biggest and most important distinction to make, however, is that *I don't have to make myself smaller* in order to lift up my sister. Period.

I can stand tall, climb high, and take her by the hand and say "Wanna come, too?" In fact, getting small to make a sister feel safe is giving her a superficial boost because the foundation of supporting her rests on a lie. The big fat lie that what God put inside of you—those treasures He perfectly placed within you and *only* you—were made to stay silent instead of shine. He didn't put that gold in you so that you'd hide it while you're around another woman. He put that gold in you so that when you let it out, it lights up the whole dang room. It lights a path for people to follow. And it gives your sister permission to unearth her gold too, and together you both light up the whole freaking world.

# 33
# Mailbox Ministry

In the past, we could only daily compare ourselves to the women in our neighborhood and social circles. But now, we have access to *millions* of people all around the world, and we don't even have to get out of bed to have access to them. Before, we had to at least get our butts out the door and walk to the mailbox to check the mail before we could start comparing. Now we don't even have to lift a finger (well, except for the one we're using to slide through our Insta feed.)

Picture this: you are depressed and anchored in bed. You are still. You are not moving.

If you are still and not moving and comparison starts generously giving out depression like candy at a parade, what do you think you will do? You're going to stay right there and not move some more and start eating the candy. Like a chubby little kid parked in front of the TV with a giant bucket of Halloween candy within arm's reach, you're going to sit there and eat and sit and eat and sit some more. Ladies, this is what we do when we stay still and we scroll through our feed. We gorge ourselves on comparison and then, almost by default, in depression.

If you were to walk outside, grab the mail, and see

Karen, your neighbor that goes on a jog at 9:00 AM every single freaking day, you'd at least have the walk from your bed to the mailbox then back to bed to distract you. And maybe on your way to the mailbox you'd have a chance to get distracted and stop and *literally* smell the roses and maybe even to get a tiny sprinkle of dopamine or vitamin D or (for the love) just some fresh air in your lungs. That's not to say you won't spiral downward from comparing yourself with Jogger Karen, but it at least gives you a fighting chance.

Unfortunately, with the advent of the smartphone and social media, the odds are stacked against us. But there are ways to climb out of the depression spiral. And I learned a lot about it through the birth of my child. What? Yep. Allow me to explain.

34
# I Mom So Fart

Did that explain anything for ya?

No? Why not? What do you mean *that section title doesn't make sense*? I mom so...*oh*. Fart. Oy vey. I wrote "fart" instead of "hard." Clearly, I don't mom so hard, at all. I brain-fart so hard. I brain-fart hard, and it stinks. But, if we really think about it, is there a difference between momming hard and brain-farting hard?

Ahem...this feels like a bad dad joke. Hopefully my editor takes it out. Because I lost half of you and the other half just fell asleep. Let's move on.

If you are a mom, or you know a mom, or you have a mom (that should cover all of us right?) stop whatever you're doing right now and send an "I see you, and you're doing great" text to a mom in your life.

Motherhood, especially at the very beginning, is such a paradoxical existence. Those first few months (or years) with babies, you are practically never alone, and yet, you can find yourself feeling more alone than you've ever felt in your life.

ESPECIALLY those first three months of motherhood (or 12 weeks, or 90 days—*however* you want to look at it) are *no joke*. For all of us new mamas, that beginning is HARD. Your entire world is turned upside-down. But like upside-down and ragdolled so hard that up is down and down is up, and with your left hand you're hanging on by one finger for dear life, and with your right hand you're holding a tiny crying human, and you haven't slept in 57 hours. Oh, and your body aches and you're probably still bleeding everywhere. But it's fine. I'm fine. We're fine.

Whether your baby is breastfed or formula-fed or fed straight manna from heaven, or whether you believe in sleep training or think it's from the Devil himself, what we all definitely have in common as moms is that we *know* sleepless nights. We know them like the back of our hand. (Notice I said hand, not pillow, because we haven't seen the front or back of our pillow since at *least* 9 months ago.)

If you go for that many days and weeks and months only sleeping for 2 to 4 hour chunks at a time, you really start losing your ever-lovin' mind. On the days that I *actually* thought I was literally losing my mind, as in going clinically insane, I tried to verbalize it to my husband for the sake of not getting trapped in my own head, and he always reminded me that studies have shown you can die a lot quicker from lack of sleep than from lack of food. For some reason, that always made me feel better. Affirmed even. Scientifically speaking, losing my mind those first three months was to be expected—it was the natural human response. I wasn't failing because I couldn't keep it together. I was just a human deprived of her most basic and essential needs for survival. I wouldn't blame a starving person for struggling, so why would I blame a sleep-deprived person?

Now mayyyybe you're a seasoned veteran mom, and you don't remember it being "*that* bad." And you're the mom who tells new moms to "Cherish when your kids are that little because you'll never get that time back."

Well, no offense, but I'd be *perfectly* content to NEVER EVER IN A MILLION YEARS return to those first three months of motherhood with my daughter. (And, you know what? If you do remember it so fondly, it's probably because in your sleep-deprived state you blocked it all out of your memory. Good job, brain! You got our backs!)

But good memories or not, it's hard. Let's all agree on that whether or not you'd ever turn the clock back.

So, now that I'm finally out of those first 3-ish months when babies literally don't produce enough of the sleep hormone melatonin to sleep for long stretches (fun fact: they start producing enough at around 10-12 weeks), I'm on the other side of things and no longer feeling like I'm dying every day. In fact, I am *loving* motherhood most days. And I have just a few, quick thoughts for mamas battling the post-baby blues. These thoughts of encouragement are NOT to make light of cases of serious postpartum depression where self-harm or harming a child is at risk. Rather, they are meant to simply give glimmers of hope for the mom with the blues; the depressed days and nights; the weeks that feel gray and lonely, as many weeks do at the very start of motherhood.

There are a few key things that I held onto tightly as a new mama who was riding the struggle bus hard. I'm going to use bullet points because, well, sometimes our brain-fart mom brains need reference ideas, not pages of information.

• I see a counselor.

This feels like a no-brainer, but sometimes we need reminded of the simplest of truths, AND we need to know that others have done it before us. We go for counseling in our house. A lot of it. It's as common as well-checks with the doctor. It's not because we can't handle life or because we are weak or because we are loonies (well, okay, maybe just a liiiittle loony). I met with a counselor the week before our baby was due. And a few months after. And literally two days ago. Change should always bring some counseling. Some of the counseling we get is preventative ("I know things are about to get hard, can you help me plan for the change so that I can adapt well?"). Some of the counseling is reactive ("Everything is HARD, I'm not adapting well, can you help me respond to this change in a more healthy way?"). We schedule regular dental cleanings for our teeth because rotting teeth are zero fun. Why can't we schedule regular counseling sessions to clean our minds, hearts and souls? Who wants to volunteer for a rotting soul? Not this girl.

• I fully entered into my sadness so that I could also fully exit from it.

My wonderful saint of a midwife gave me some of the best advice anyone could ever give a new mother: the more you resist the sadness, the harder and stronger it pushes back. We have GOT to stop trying to hold it together. Which brings me to my next point…

• I let the tears flow like a river. Or like a waterfall. Or like freaking Hurricane Irma.

Two of my closest friends (who were moms years before I had my first) lovingly let me in on glimpses of their early motherhood. Their stories helped prepare me. One told me about how her hormones were so all over the place post-birth that while she was nursing, sometimes tears would just start flowing and she would have no idea why she was crying. Another friend told me all she did was cry for the majority of the first three months of motherhood. *Three months of crying*, then she adapted. And everything was fine. Cry as often as you need to. I remember thinking the more I cried the better. It was like detoxing my system.

• I learned to know my warning signs and to know when I need to tap out.

This is, yet again, advice I got from a mom friend who was a mom long before I was. Don't be a hero. If you are blessed to have Dad around and you're seeing warning signs that you're not thinking clearly… WAKE. HIM. UP. Wake him when you need to take 5 (or 45), even if it's 4 AM. If you're falling asleep with a newborn in your arms, or if bouncing the baby to sleep starts to cross the line into jumping jacks-ing the baby to sleep, it's time to call for backup. It's better to have you and Baby stay safe than to power through dangerous exhaustion. Single moms, this is the part where I just sit down and bury my face in my hands because I have no words. You all are the real MVPs. I can't even begin to wrap my head around what you experience. But the same principle applies: know when to ask for help. Call a relative. Call a neighbor. Call someone. Asking for help isn't you being weak, its you being a good mother.

• I made my village one text away.

I have a small handful of trusted mom-friends who I can share "words of the wind" with. This is a fun term from Job, a book in the Bible, that's basically referring to "crap you say when you're not thinking clearly." When I first became a mom, I had a group text going with four of my closest mom-friends who I could say virtually anything to in a completely judgment-free zone. I can't tell you how many times I sent things like "I feel like I'm drowning" (except add a few choice four letter words sprinkled in there). And they wouldn't attempt to preach me out of it. They just let me be there. They were just with me. They reminded me how much better it gets after the first three months. They sympathized. They offered to come over and hold my baby so I could nap for 20 minutes. It was amazing.

• I answer honestly.

When people ask you, "How's motherhood going?!" or, "How do you like being a mom?", it's FINE if you answer honestly. In fact, that's the only way you *should* answer. It's such a sad thing to know that 99.999999% of moms are experiencing the same heartache and exhaustion, yet typically all we do or see from each other are the cute social media pictures and the put-together-self at church Sunday mornings. I can't tell you how many times I answered those questions with things like, "Umm…it's both terrible and amazing," only to be stared at awkwardly. Well, guess what? This tiny human IS amazing. And yes I love her SO much. However, never sleeping and bleeding everywhere ARE terrible. The point is to be *authentic*.

Don't try to be the mom who's always "Good!", "Great!", "My babies are my world/life/everything!", "I just made homemade baby food while simultaneously cleaning a toilet AND shaving my legs!" Ha! That mom? She doesn't exist. And the sooner you can accept that, the sooner you will love the mother you actually are.

• I take preventative routine breaks.

So often we don't communicate needing a hand until we've bottled up all of our exhaustion, frustration, sadness and anger for so long that we explode–whether "exploding" means anger and rage or lying lifeless on a bed of tears eating an entire tub of ice cream/buying an entire clothing store in one day. We've *all* experienced some degree of our own mom-plosion. (Unless you haven't…then God bless you. Also...are you secretly a robot? Mother Theresa? Jesus Himself?) The point is, we all have our breaking point. But if we proactively ask for help as a ROUTINE part of our day—yes, even on the days we feel like Wonder Woman and we are ON it—we accomplish two things:

First, we practice asking for help when we aren't overwhelmed, making it much easier to ask for help efficiently (and kindly) when we *are* overwhelmed.

Second, we can step away and refill our tanks *preventatively* on a regular basis so that we rarely end up in a sticky situation and running on empty (aka punching walls and tearing apart chairs, or on the floor sobbing uncontrollably...not that I've ever done either of those things...okay maybe I have). It's kind of the same mentality that says you should fill up your gas tank at a quarter tank instead of when it's on E. This can look different for all of us depending on what our lives and daily routines look like, but here's an example of what it looks like in our household: my husband gets our daughter out of bed every morning. He goes in, and it's the sweetest thing to hear from another room: they say good mornings, snuggle and giggle and sing, and he changes her diaper. This not only gives her a consistent sweet time with her dad before he leaves for work, but it also helps me start my day with calm. I get to sit on the couch and read or think or pray or just stare at a wall for 5-15 minutes. He also does bath time almost every night with her, and *again* I use this time to go for a walk, chat with friends, sit and close my eyes, WHATEVER. I just get a breather after a long day of mom-ing. The tricky part with these things is to see them as gift-offerings, not hard and fast rules. If for some reason he's running behind one morning or schedules just don't work out, I don't want to get stuck feeling bitter and angry that he didn't "hold up his end of the deal." Rather, we are constantly looking for ways to give each other gifts—gifts of special one-on-one time with our daughter, and gifts of getting a breather. If he's had a particularly stressful day and I can tell he needs some time to himself after work, I have asked in the past if he wants me to do bath time. Normally he does it anyway, regardless of the kind of day he's had, but my offer means a lot to him. And his offers mean the world to me. I have gotten in the habit of communicating something like, "It would be really great for me right now if you helped me preventatively protect my sanity." And he gets it. He knows that means that I'm seeing warning signs of stress and need a breather.

• I do my best to love my mind well by what I eat.

This one is HARD, friends. And it may just become a full on book on its own because it really can make a huge impact. The food we eat really does affect our mental well-being. Like, on so many levels. So, I won't get into this one because I'll save it for another day so I can show you some cool science to back it all up and encourage you, as well as some initial first steps you could try out. But just try to love yourself well by the food you eat at least 90% of the time. If right now loving yourself well means embracing that left over 10% by eating the moose tracks in the freezer, no one's judging. I get it. Eat the ice cream.

# 35
# Girl, Let Me Love You

*"You cannot persuade a depressed person that he has not been utterly rejected by God if he is persuaded that he has been. But you can stand by him. And you can keep soaking him in the benevolence, mercy, goodness, and sympathy of Jesus."*
*- John Piper, "When the Darkness Will not Lift."*

When I was really depressed, my friend Lauren didn't send me texts with scripture or buy me books on emotional management or even try to convince me not to be depressed. Instead, she did three really really life-changing things:

She would ask me if I had eaten yet that day, and when the answer was almost always no, she would bring me a snack. Omelettes and apples dipped in peanut butter will always hold a special place in my heart because of her.

She would call me on the days when I couldn't get out of bed, and knowing I wouldn't answer the phone because talking was too hard, she would leave me a voicemail saying, "I just wanted you to hear my voice telling you I love you. God loves you. No matter what you're feeling right now, you are beautiful, you are loved, and I'm so thankful for you."

She invited me over to watch a movie with her, she

came over and asked me to walk around outside with her (which would sometimes turn into us playing outside like little kids), she sat with me in silence, she did my dishes. She just existed with me.

There are a select few people, like Lauren, who I cannot thank enough for how they never gave up on me. Like my husband, Ricky, who quite literally held me like a baby some days and let me cry on his chest. He didn't tell me to get over it. He didn't tell me to man up. He let me cry as long as I needed to. He prayed over me when I didn't have the strength to pray myself. Like my brother and his wife Alina, who somedays, would pick me up on my most teary days just to paint with them—they didn't demand I explain myself or even talk at all. They just sat with me and we painted pictures together, sprawled out on their living room floor. Another friend, Emily, drew up a cute menu for me with food options to pick from on a day that I felt immobilized by sadness sitting on her back porch wondering what I believed and questioning who I was.

There are too many stories to tell. But the point is that others' tender care for me and their "just existing" with me without any real agenda told me so much more than words ever could have. It told me I was loved and wanted just the way I was. And to feel loved, truly loved and wanted without any need to impress or produce, is the most important part of healing. And being truly loved and accepted *before* we heal is often the thing that nudges us toward healing in the first place.

## 36
# Out of Hiding

The greatest temptation for me when I'm depressed (or honestly just having a really crap day) is to hide. It's my default response if I don't catch myself as I'm thinking, *Today is too messy, I am too messy. I don't want anyone to see me in this mess.* But when I think like that, what I'm *actually* believing at my core is that I am too hard to love today, so I don't want to burden anyone with trying to love me. On those messy days, when I believe I'm unlovable and I have canceled on friends because of it, do you know how much I am robbing from everyone involved? So, so much.

Just the other day, I had plans with my friend Martha and at least five times I opened my phone to cancel with her because my day got messy quick and I was spiraling. My daughter was throwing savage animal tantrums about everything under the sun like only two year-olds can. I hadn't taken a shower yet or gotten out of sweatpants (or even brushed my teeth. I know, gross). But we all needed some fresh air because winter cabin fever is REAL and I wondered if it would help my daughter. So I took her and our puppy for what I *thought* would be a quick walk. Before I realized it, we had gone too far, I was late to meet Martha at my house, the temperature was dropping quickly, my daughter was crying and asking to be held, and I was crying. Everyone was crying. I opened my phone to finally send that cancellation text but realized she was already at my house because we were late getting back. She told me she was parked in the driveway waiting for us. I was so embarrassed. But I took in a big shaky breath and said, "Martha, I'm so sorry. Can you come pick us up? We're all crying and cold and stranded in the middle of the neighborhood." And of course she came and found us and we piled into her warm car and drove home together. Not only was I riding the hot mess express, I literally had to humble myself and say, "I need your help."

The beautiful thing is that our friendship reached a new level that day. She didn't see my messy house or my messy heart. She saw *me*. And because she saw me, she felt safe to let herself be seen too. We talked about everything we could possibly talk about over hot tea and a toddler bouncing back and forth between us. What started out as the coldest, grayest, most overwhelming day all winter became one of my favorite winter days, with more warmth and freedom than any sunshine could have ever given me.

## 37
# The Spring of Sisterhood

Lately, I've been reminding myself that as sisters we hold such a privileged and pivotal place in each other's worlds. The women next to me will do one of two things in my presence: they will either shut down and feel smaller around me or they will breathe deep and stand taller next to me. I want them to do the latter. I want to be the kind of sister that says, "I'm safe. I know my worth. *You* take the stage this time, sister. Stand tall, don't get small. I won't let you shrink or go silent anymore. The world needs both of our voices."

I'm trying not to hide anymore, no matter how loveable I do (or *don't*) feel. I'm cancelling on friends less. I'm welcoming my sisters into all my mess. And that invitation is springing up all kinds of life even in the dead of winter.

**Strip Off: Lonewolf Living**

My sassy friend Sarah gives fantastic, straightforward fashion advice. Sometimes, in a group text with a few friends, we'll send pictures back and forth while shopping to get each other's input. A few of us have tried on some pretty terrible things, and the classic Sarah response to that type of outfit is "GET THAT OFF YOUR BODY RIGHT NOW." This is precisely what I tell myself and what I want to tell *you.* Sisters, we've got to strip off our isolation, our perfectionism, and our comparison. Trust me, it's not your color. So, GET THAT OFF YOUR BODY.

**Step Into: Authentic friendships.**

Literally "step into" your friend's messy house and heart (and let her step into yours). Organic relationships are worth the extra cost.

**GV Fashion Tip**

My friend Amy and I are always joking around about our #soulsista outfits, area rugs, book titles, and dreams. We often end up dreaming up related ideas or ordering the same area rug without even knowing the other is doing it. We frequently text each other outfit ideas too, *and* we've both played significant roles in helping each other launch our first books (she's actually the mastermind behind all of our fun outfit illustrations! Thanks, Ame!).

What if instead of competing with one another in our fashion choices, our home decor, or our dreams, we teamed up more? What if instead of flinching when we end up wearing the same outfit, we laughed about it and took #soulsista #twinkie pictures to celebrate? Today's fashion tip is to share your fashion with your sisters—maybe even shop your girlfriend's closet and let her shop yours! It's so much more fun to brainstorm outfits together or swap out clothes than it is to shop alone.

*The best-dressed woman is the one that walks next to her sisters.*

# ADDICTION

# 38
# Average Addicts

Here's what I want to tell you about addictions:

I know essentially nothing about them. I have a lot of them. You might have some. And neither of us likes to admit they are real, let alone talk about them.

That about covers it.

I totally get that a section on addictions is kind of a buzzkill. And I'm not going to be talking about the times that I smoked weed, saw my boyfriend tripping on acid, or got so drunk I probably should've had my stomach pumped. This is about the addictions I have that I didn't want to admit were addictions. These are the addictions so many of us live with, but we normalize them and then we feel justified in our judgments of the people in rehab because they are the "real addicts."

What I want you to hear is that I found out my addictions were keeping me small. Really small. They were keeping me from being the person I was created to be. That's why they are worth digging in to. That's why they are worth fighting. Addictions are *not* about God wagging his finger down at us from heaven; they are about prisons we get stuck in. And they truly are prisons, whether they be big or small. So, basically this section is a list of all of my personal prisons. But I hope that hearing the stories about me breaking out of my prison cells will help you believe that the freedom that comes with that is worth asking, *What am I addicted to? And if I do indeed happen to be human and have some addictions, how can I lovingly punch those addictions in the face?*

Because you are worth it. *I* am worth it.

Because I don't want an addiction to be the thing that keeps me small, keeps me from freedom.

Because seeing my addiction for what it is is a form of loving myself and the people around me.

That is all.

Here we go.

## 39
# So What Even IS Addiction?

"[Addiction] originates in a human being's desperate attempt to solve a problem: the problem of emotional pain, of overwhelming stress, of lost connection, of loss of control, of a deep discomfort with the self. In short, it is a forlorn attempt to solve the problem of human pain. Hence my mantra: 'The question is not why the addiction, but why the pain.'"-Dr. Gabor Mate

*Thanks, Doc.*

I hope you didn't think *I* was going to try answering that question. It's such a complex thing to answer, and I'm sure there are so many ways you could answer it. But we'll run with his answer for now.

So: We feel pain. We are willing to take on more pain in order to not feel the early pain. But because we never really took care of the first pain, it's a vicious cycle—numbing ourselves into ash so that we won't have to address the deep early wounds.

## 40
# Boys

I feel so embarrassed to admit this. I've been sitting here, trying to come up with a collection of words that won't make me sound ridiculous or shallow...but I guess it wouldn't be an addiction if it was easy for me to talk about.

Up until I was 19 years old (and then some), my entire life was motivated by, moved according to, and made up of boys. I cared very little about anything else. I wish I could tell you *why* I was obsessed; I know it sounds like I'm being dramatic, but it wasn't just a case of the classic teenage girl obsessed with her crush who doodles hearts all over her notebook during math class. I mean that I genuinely did not care about anything in my life besides getting the attention of men. Ugh. Guys, this is embarrassing.

I am sure a counselor could evaluate me and say that it came from any number of things: I was the first girl in my small fifth grade class to start her period at the tender age of 10 years old. That also means I was the first girl to have hips and boobs. We could blame it on that at least *partially*, I'm sure. I had hormones that most girls don't have to deal with that early, and I probably started getting attention from boys earlier than some girls because, well, boobs. I'm sure that became a self-fulfilling prophecy to some degree—I was confused and none of my friends could relate, so I felt really alone in it all. I'm also convinced that the earlier you get attention from boys, the earlier you start getting addicted to it. I was at such a formative age and constantly asking myself, "WHAT EVEN are all these feelings? WHO am I?? WHAT is happeniiiiing?" When I started getting answers to those questions from boys in the form of staring, flirting, or butt-grabs, it's easy to see how I could start to mold myself around those parameters.

I also think it's important to note that we learn to value what our parents value. We learn to invest energy in what our parents invest energy into. But it's not a conscious effort, of course; it just happens. It's the reason you fold clothes a certain way, wash dishes a certain way, or host people in your home in a particular manner. What we see our parents doing *habitually* becomes our framework for how we live our lives, at least until we get old enough and self-aware enough to start choosing our own path.

When you grow up with divorced parents, it's such a different dynamic than growing up with married parents. I am not saying one is always better than the other—I know that some marriages are so toxic the damage would be far worse on the kids than a divorce. I get that. But when your parents are married, you might see them love each other, ignore each other, or fight with each other. But you *don't* see them single, in the dating game.

That means you probably saw them fill their time with regular life. Maybe you saw them mowing the lawn, maybe you saw them involved in community outreach/ their church, maybe you saw them going out with friends. Maybe you saw them reading books, or working on house projects or preparing presentations for work, pursuing dreams or planting gardens. Whatever you saw them do, it built your understanding of what humans ought to fill their time with. These are all things that I can't, for the life of me, remember *ever* seeing my parents do.

Here's what I remember: I remember them wanting to soak up time with me and my brothers because they each only had us for two weeks out of the month. And I remember seeing them date. Can you imagine? The dating season of life is pretty all-consuming. You forget the rest of the world exists. We've all had seasons where we've had to apologize to a friend for ditching them one too many times because a new significant other rolled around, or we've seen friends fall off the face of the earth when they enter into a new relationship. Now just imagine that on top of that all-consuming season of life, you have children to take care of. That's hard. I don't blame my parents. There's no blueprint on how to do it, and I can't say that I would have done it any better myself if I was in their shoes.

And again, remember they each only had us for 50% of our lives. Can you imagine knowing you only get to spend half of your kids' childhood with them? They had us *every other week*, so we basically got used to each of our parents' world's being put on pause in order to be with us whenever we switched houses. Not only chores but friends, social life, bills, hobbies—everything got put on hold to be done next week so they could devote all of their time and attention to their kids.

It's also important to note that it's not that my parents *didn't* do interesting things—my mom and dad are actually fascinating people. They just didn't do the fascinating things around us very often because, like I said, they were either wanting to soak up the little time they had with us or dating someone.

For example, as a single mom, my momma slowly got her master's degree over the span of five years, but I don't remember seeing her study or work on assignments even *once*. It really is honorable, the way she did it. She always waited until we were asleep, and then she would work late into the night, or she would wait until the weeks we were at my dad's house to study and get caught up on homework. My dad got his PHD in IO Psychology and often traveled all over the world for work but only on the weeks we were with my mom. He also served at our Church and occasionally played basketball Sunday nights with a group of guys when we weren't with him.

I do remember my mom taking in children from other countries who needed foster parents in the U.S. in order to have medical procedures done. I think it's part of why I now have an interest in being a foster parent myself—I saw that lifestyle modeled, and the openness to those in need with which my mom ran our home. I also remember seeing my dad wake up early every morning to have quiet meditation time with his journal and his prayer books which I think is why its been easy for me to incorporate a similar ritual into my daily life.

My parents were incredible parents in so many ways, but they were also very lonely parents. I don't think we were made to be alone like they were (let alone raise children alone. And I don't just mean romantically alone but even alone without community. We know this, don't we? We've heard "it takes a village" a thousand times. But we lived thousands of miles away from the rest of our family due to a pre-divorce cross-country move for my dad to get his PhD. This meant that on top of my parents only hanging out with friends on weeks they didn't have us kids, they had no aunts or uncles or cousins or grandparents to help carry the load and provide a support system.

Divorce is messy. Nothing about it screams "optimal way to live." I saw them oftentimes trying to escape loneliness. That means that while some kids were learning to fold laundry or have healthy relationships as they mimicked their parents (along with the beautiful things I learned from them), I was picking up on how to run fast from loneliness into the arms of other people.

## 41
# Thesis

So what's the silver lining? Being loved and wanted is a very good, natural thing, so how did I eventually learn to be loved and wanted in a healthy way while being content within myself and not looking for some guy to fulfill my needs, loneliness, or emptiness?

Well, first off, like pretty much everything in this book, I am not a pro. I am figuring this all out right alongside you.

But here's the cliffnotes version of it:

I hit rock bottom my senior year of high school. After I stopped drinking and partying, I was completely alone. Isolated. Removed from my old friends.

Then I met and dated a different sort of guy. He wasn't the class king, or a jock, or even popular. He was, at times, actually homeless and hopeless. He had a very hard upbringing as well—the kind of upbringing I wouldn't wish on a worst enemy. I swung really hard on the opposite side of the pendulum: every other guy I had dated before him was borderline (or not so borderline) abusive, aggressive, and assertive...the kind of guy you don't want to piss off because, well, he's got people in high places and muscles and too much testosterone. This time, I dated someone who carried himself even smaller than I did. He needed protection and to be nurtured, and it drew me in. I am sure it felt safer this way. If I was the stronger, more stable one, well, it was (in theory) harder to get hurt that way.

My family took him in. I even turned down a scholarship at a university so that I could help him go to a community college because the only way he could go to school was if I drove him there. So I completely rearranged my entire life to make that happen.

Now.

Remember when I said my parents were incredible, even if they were hurting?

My dad swooped in and made a *very* tough call...but a call that changed the trajectory of the rest of my life in the best way possible. The day before classes started at that university I'd gotten into but had turned down for the sake of my boyfriend, my dad "forced" me to leave the community college a week into classes and to not only attend the university but to move into the dorms *completely* removed from the guy I was dating.

Obviously, I threw a tantrum. How could he separate us?! I protested—it was *cruel and unusual punishment*! I *loved* my boyfriend with all of my shattered, beat up, confused heart. But deep down, there was a tiny, hopeful whisper in me. I didn't want to admit it, but I was so thankful my dad was fighting for me. I was thankful he stepped in and said, "Even if you don't see your worth right now, *I* see it. If you won't fight for you, *I will.* I won't sit here and watch you throw your life away for some guy."

*Throw my life away... for some guy.*

If I had a thesis statement to describe the first 19 years of my life, that's what it would be. It's what I repeatedly did. That's why I consider it an addiction: I was repeatedly going to something (or someone) to fulfill my needs and aching soul...even if over and over again the thing/person was destructive to me.

## 42
# Spiritual Awakening

My freshman year of college was much less train-wrecky (yeah, that's a word now) than my four years of high school, but it was still pretty messy.

I was trying to grow as a person and be "spiritual," but I had no idea what that even meant.

So, since boys were the one thing I thought I couldn't live without, and I was trying to grow as a person, I went on a dating fast that supposedly was going to last for......wait for it....... FOUR. YEARS. (HA!) This is the extreme, all or nothing kind of person I was. It was either ALL the boys 24/7, or NONE of them for the next century.

Even though I was pretty terrible at my dating fast, the good news is that I stopped giving my body away to people I thought I loved. I had no serious boyfriends my entire freshman year (baby steps!), and it was a miracle from above. But that didn't mean I wasn't still *talking* to several boys at once. I don't know what kids call it these days—maybe it's "lit" or "fire" or "shipping," but when I was 18, we called it "talking." That means you are literally talking (and maybe making out sometimes) with someone but not officially "together." I did my best not to make out too much, but I was definitely talking, leading on, and even hurting a number of guys at once. It feels really yucky to say that. But all addictions are yucky.

Stick with me here, guys. Everything is about to change.

I was hanging out with one of the guys I was "talking" with at a cafe on campus, and a friend of his from spanish class walked up to us: tall, dark, and so sexy. Oh, and speaking Spanish. It's important to note that as a Cuban American girl growing up in the midwest, seeing a guy my age speaking spanish was like spotting a rare species of exotic animal you can only *dream* of seeing in real life. I really tried to play it cool, but inside I was all "BE STILL MY LATIN OVARIES."

A few weeks later, I couldn't get this spanish-speaking-sexy-man out of my head. I was *really* trying on this dating fast, you guys! And... by "trying" I mean checking his facebook every five minutes to see if he had accepted my friend request (turned out, he'd given up Facebook for Lent. OH, OKAY. So he's hot *and* holy. *Hubba-hubba-ding-ding come to mama!* Sorry. Too much? Probably. I should stop...). One day while checking his Facebook *again*, I came across a few important pictures that I was positive were a sign we were meant to be together: a picture of him holding his mom's hand while dancing (*loves his mama AND loves dancing?! BLESS*), a picture of him playing guitar and singing (*swoooooon*), and a picture of him wearing a cool wooden cross (remember, I was *trying* to be spiritual, so seeing this felt like a win even if I didn't really know anything about his spirituality). Since I couldn't get in touch with him like a civilized person would over Facebook and we still had something like 31 looong days of Lent left, I started doing the unthinkable: I tried to befriend him *in person* (gasp!).

I started asking around to see if anyone knew him. Lots of people did, and the he-said-she-saids circulating about this mystery-no-facebook-man started making their way to me. He lived at *this* dorm and liked to eat at *that* cafe. He was involved in *this* campus organization and went to *that* high school. And so on. The one that really sealed the deal for me, though, was when I heard through the grapevine that he'd broken up with a high school girlfriend because he wanted to wait to have sex until he got married and she didn't. *That* was the record scratch for me—um, excuse me, *what*?! I didn't know why he would want that. I didn't really believe it when I heard it, and I didn't even know if I liked it all that much. I was just intrigued. Because I had never ever *ever* in my life heard of that actually happening, let alone a guy wanting to wait on his own accord. It pulled me in, though, the romance of it all. That was the only thing I ever really felt guys actually wanted. What if this guy was different?

I started eating at the cafe I'd heard he ate at. I started changing my walking routes hoping to run in to him. In retrospect, was I stalking him, at least a little bit? No. No way. Of course not. Well...okay maybe. A little. Yes. The answer is yes.

And my plan worked! I started running into him! Before I knew it, we were having lunch together all the time between classes. We had group jam sessions with friends where a friend of mine suggested we all exchange numbers (she was being a sweet friend and basically everyone exchanged numbers just so that Ricky and I could get each other's number. Smooth, sister, *smoooooth.*).

As it turned out, he was *also* on a dating fast. Ha! What were the odds!? Only his was a *real* one. Mine was born out of confusion, self-discovery, and mostly (if I'm being perfectly honest) guilt. His was born out of love. He loved God. A *lot.* And He just wanted time to focus on Him. Which honestly, at first, was endearing to me, but also sounded kinda crazy. I was raised in a church but didn't really know what loving God (and not just being afraid of Him) could even look like. But God knew that it would take a *boy*—the thing I worshipped most—to show me how that kind of "god" will always fall short. What happened in the weeks to come was basically the spiritual equivalent of Ricky, that sexy spanish-speaking tall dark and handsome mystery man, taking himself off of my boy-worshipping altar and saying (in Spanish, of course), "I'll never be able to fill all your needs" and then pointing to the One who could. And it was so dang beautiful.

Whether you believe in God or not, the reality is that people will never be able to fulfill each other completely. That's way too much pressure on a human, and we weren't created to carry that kind of weight. We will *always* feel let down if we're counting on a person to meet all our needs. We have to find that fulfillment from within and from something (or Someone) bigger than ourselves. Something that doesn't bend with the wind whenever it blows. I can't be rooted in something so unreliable. To me that *something* bigger, *something* unchanging, *something* completely fulfilling, is God.

It's been about eleven years since I really wrapped my head around that, and I'm still figuring out what it all means, a little more every day.

43

# My Diagnosis

If I would have been tested earlier, I would have likely been on them for a decade. I was 22 years old and had been on antidepressants for three years. They got me out of a dangerous place, and for that I'm so very thankful. However, while I was on them, while I was *functioning* most days, I wasn't actually happy, and I was *definitely* not healthy. I didn't fully realize that until my first year of marriage stirred the pot enough to make it oh so very painfully obvious.

What's the best way to find out you're *not really* okay? Go ahead and move in with someone. Oh, but don't just move in; "become one" with them. Exchange forever vows (and geez, how little do you know what you're signing up for when you say, "For better or for worse"?). Sure, on your wedding night your clothes hit the floor, but it's the following weeks and months that really undress you fully. The beginning of marriage in and of itself is always hard. Living with someone is like a mirror reflecting back all the crap in your heart that you didn't even know was there. When you live alone, you just kind of get used to your own dysfunction—it becomes normal. But then you move in and what used to be "normal" and okay when you lived alone (like, oh, you know, staying in bed all day and not showing up for obligations like work or family events) suddenly shows itself as really *not* normal when your husband is confused about why you didn't go to work *again* and confronts you on it.

Where in my wedding vows did I warn my husband that in a few short months he would be in an *actual car chase* with his wife, risking a serious speeding ticket while chasing her down the streets of our small town making sure she didn't drive her car off a cliff or just keep driving all the way to Mexico? Oh yes, folks. I was a real class act. That actually happened. Unfortunately, there's no magic pill a doctor can prescribe along with your depression meds that gives you conflict management skills.

*Oh, so healthy conflict management doesn't involve me running away from life and peeling out of our driveway? Shoot. I guess I should've actually read those marriage books we were supposed to read for premarital counseling.* And I should note that Ricky read them *all*. I, on the other hand, would ask him to give me the cliff notes as we drove to our premarital counseling sessions with our pastor. This basically sums up our marriage.

It's nearly impossible to hide all your ugly, all your tears, all your fears and failings...but mostly, it's impossible to hide your insecurities and depression. Eventually, if you aren't healthy, you will have a breakdown...and that I did. So many times.

My breakdowns looked like (and these are all real events that happened in our first year of marriage): a car chase, bailing on commitments as I stayed in bed for the fourth day in a row, breaking a favorite piece of furniture, cold eyes and a cold heart that lay like a stormcloud over our house, ugly crying and silent tears (that came randomly and too often and then stayed too long). And then, sometimes, all of this was replaced by a lifelessness that made me feel like a zombie with no emotion at all.

On one fateful rare sunny afternoon when I was feeling mostly good and emotionally balanced, my tired husband asked me to sit down on the porch with him to talk. I got a little sweaty (do you get the nervous sweats too?) as I knew from his tone that this talk wouldn't be a fun one. We sat down, and he looked me in the eyes with pain in his face and said gently but desperately, "Something needs to change. I don't know what exactly. But we can't live like this." He knew that this bright sunny day wasn't normal—that we were just in the eye of the latest hurricane of depression.

As embarrassing as it is to admit, I realized that day that there was a part of me deep deep down that didn't really want to get better. Not because I liked being miserable! I hate that part. But because I found *comfort* in the diagnosis. I felt security, and I even found pieces of my identity in it. My medical diagnosis of clinical depression helped explain so much that I started to own it—I remember I used to call it "*my* depression." "My depression is really bad today," I would think to myself or tell someone. I would carry it around like I would an expensive purse and use it as an emotional crutch. In a way, I was addicted to the parameters that my diagnosis set for me—I would not push myself to go for a walk when I was stuck in bed because, what's the use? This is who I am and how I am wired! How could something like a walk affect the chemical imbalance in my brain?

Diagnoses are such beautiful tools, but like any tool they are easily misused. Hilary Mcbride uses the phrase, "Name it to tame it." I absolutely love that—you can't possibly get better if you don't tame the beast first. But it's not that we name it to *stay* with it, letting it take over our lives. We name it to *tame* it.

It hit me like a ton of bricks: all I'd ever done since the moment I was diagnosed was assume depression was as much a part of me as the color of my eyes. I had never even given God the space to heal me. I had never *asked*. I had never given myself the space to have hope.

I didn't want to assume I knew His plan for me, and I

was open to whatever: medication, no medication, magical instant faith healing, a lifetime of heavy-heartedness-but-maybe-He-could-use-my-suffering-for-good...or maybe, just *maybe*, a life of health, wellness, and getting off this depression roller coaster(?).

I remember feeling embarrassed when I asked God for healing, like an ashamed child who won't look her dad in the eyes because it feels silly to ask for a miracle: "God... hi. I know you heal sometimes, and sometimes you choose not to. But I figured it wouldn't hurt to ask. Can you take this away?"

It was quite literally faith the size of a mustard seed. Maybe even a poppy seed. I was fearful and doubtful. But I still asked.

Ricky and I felt confident that God would want me to be involved in my healing and that He'd provide tools for healing if it was His will. At the time we didn't know how deep that truth went, but we had a hunch and that was enough to get us started. So we prayed and made a plan. I talked to my doctor, a mentor, and a nurse, and then did some reading, praying, and dreaming on my own.

I was going to wean off of my medication slowly over a 3 month period—a 90-day experiment in mental health and healing (in retrospect, it could and should have been a much slower, longer process, but we were taking risks and stumbling forward). We planned for a long enough period of time for life to still happen to us, for me to be confronted with the inevitable ups and downs of life so that I could practice healthy coping as my medication decreased.

Over the 90 days our plan was to count the amount of times I faced "unmanageable emotions." We labeled them this way because I didn't want to feel like I was being tested and had to have a smile on my face for 90 days, or that I wasn't allowed to ever be sad or else I had somehow "failed" the test. I knew that human emotion was healthy—it's only when the emotion becomes consistently *unmanageable* or removes my ability to function daily and brings along irrational behavior or thought patterns that it tiptoes across the line into illness.

We designed a carefully crafted tool box of self-care goals every day during those 90 days in hopes of replacing the chemicals I was no longer getting from medication. It's a tool box I still use every day of my life, and over time God has even given me more tools to add to the box along with a deeper understanding of depression.

To start piecing together my toolbox, we used the rocks-in-the-sand analogy that a mentor had counseled me with. In a nutshell, it goes like this: in order to fit big rocks *and* sand in a jar, the rocks would need to go in first, and then the sand could fill in around them—if you try to put the sand in first, there would be no space left for the rocks. I asked God to help me see what my "big rocks" were: the things I needed to prioritize for my day, every day, for healing and balance—and then I could fit the sand in (the lesser priority things) on top of those "rocks."

My first rock was *Scripture*. I thought of it this way: every morning we put on two outfits. One is made out of fabric (our actual clothes) and the other is made out of thoughts and beliefs (our "internal clothes"). Nine times out of ten we only choose the outfit we slip onto our skin, but we aren't aware of the outfit we wear on our souls. I knew depression made my soul-outfit look a lot like this: "Nothing fits me well, I look ugly, I am too messy, no one likes me, I can't do this, I am too complicated to love." So I wanted to have truth that I slipped on my soul every morning before depression had a chance to dress me for the day.

The second rock I'd prioritize for my life-jar was *Community*. When I was depressed my number one biggest temptation was to hide. Stay isolated. Hide from others and not let anyone in. So we decided to punch that hiding in the face (always with the face punching) and make one of my big rocks some type of contact with a friend every day. I had a group of four dear friends who I let in on the plan. They checked in on me often, and I did my best to be brave and send them a message when everything in me was telling me to stay far away from people.

I called the third daily rock *"Good Eats"*. At the time, I didn't know a whole lot about nutrition. I just knew that when I was depressed, I either didn't eat at all or only wanted donuts (and lots of 'em). And I had an inkling (after googling for an entire 15 seconds) that donuts were probably not making me feel very good. That was enough to at least *try* to eat better. Plus, you know, health and hippies and yada-yada-yada. (Little did I know I'd later become a hippie health nut myself.)

The final rock was *Exercise*. Ugh. This one was actual torture. Exercise was not my jam (which is funny in retrospect given that I later became a personal trainer who owned her own health coaching company for four years. Welp, we all have to start somewhere!). I knew you were supposed to experience "endorphins" or a "runner's high" or *whatever*, so I figured it would help. The exercise rock was just 30 minutes of an "elevated heart rate" once a day (this is how fancy my exercise terms were back then, you guys). Some days, that meant breaking a sweat playing tennis or going on a good run. Other days, though, that meant riding a stationary bike on the slowest, easiest setting for 30 minutes while watching a movie.

This wasn't a perfect formula. But it was a start.

(Real quick spoiler alert for you: after the 90 days, we evaluated my episodes of unmanageable emotions—I had two short-lasting episodes during the first 60 days and then zero during the last 30 days.)

By the end of it I felt balanced, capable of feeling both joy and healthy sadness, and stable for a consistent enough amount of time that we felt at peace with the decision to stay off of meds. By a doctor's standards, I was no longer depressed (insert party hat emoji here!).

But friends, here is the most important thing I want you to hear about this healing journey of mine. God chose it. His healing can come in so many forms. If I would have stayed on meds, I don't think that would indicate a lack of healing but rather a route for healing that I hadn't asked for but was willing and open to. It would have been healing nonetheless.

However, His will for me was to have daily freedom from depression and to do it without medication. He continues to choose renewed healing for me every single day, and I keep saying yes to that invite.

What I love about the 90 days is that I didn't do it perfectly. There were days where I missed one of the big rocks, which makes my healing all the more profound. If I would have done it perfectly I could say that on my own strength and strategy, I was healed. But it wasn't perfect, and I was healed regardless. God wanted me to embrace the tools He's offered for health and join him in the dance to freedom. He didn't want me to just be an observer, watching life happen to me, but rather a participant, involved in the writing of my own story. God doesn't ask for our perfection during our healing journey. He just wants our participation because participation is teamwork and teamwork is incredibly intimate and intimacy is what He wants with us.

He could easily choose a less intimate method like the "Almighty Cosmic Forklift", letting us lie there while He scoops us right up with zero effort or response on our part. And sometimes, I think there actually are moments where He does that sort of thing. But I think that most of the time He prefers to come right next to us as we lie in the grave, to reach His hand out and touch us. It's the extending our hand in response to His that makes it such a tender moment. He loves when we respond to Him. I absolutely think physical touch is one of His love languages. He wants to touch our hand and breathe life into our skin.

*Taking her by the hand he said to her, "Talitha cumi," which means, "Little girl, I say to you, arise." And immediately the girl got up and began walking, and they were immediately overcome with amazement.*

*- Mark 5:41–42*

This girl was pronounced dead. DEAD, ya'll. And simply with the touch of her hand and two words, Jesus brought her back to life. Notice He could have just as easily spoken at an arm's length away, and she would have been healed all the same. But he chose to come near and take her by the hand, and *then* He spoke those words and healed her.

I know I've said it a hundred times, but I always try to speak from a place that lets you be where you're at, not assuming that you and I believe in the same God. But this story was really hard to tell without being totally transparent with you guys about what I believe. I was imprisoned by my diagnosis, and I was set free by faith the size of a poppy seed.

# 44
# Little Pills and Mountain Tops

When I was a senior in high school, I was placed in a math class with all sophomores partially on my choosing and partially on my teacher's suggestion because I had barely scraped by in the previous math class. I say that not to make myself sound like a terrible student who hardly ever studied and graduated high school on prayer and note-passing to friends alone (all of that is precisely what happened though—you guys, I was figuring it out, okay?! Don't judge!), but I tell you this to set the stage for a quick essay on…(dramatic pause)...SCIENCE.

Yes. If you just threw up in your mouth a little (as I typically would) at the mention of math or science (where my right-brained sistas at?!), don't go skipping this one just yet because I promise you want to read this one. I am going to skip the fancy-pants jargon you don't need to hear and tell you exactly what actually matters here. Oh, and if you do get pumped at the mention of science, I fully believe you will ascend into heaven on your last day as the holiest of us all. God bless you. Also, pray for me. I still count with my fingers.

First let's define a couple important mental health/ science buzzwords:

Serotonin: A chemical referred to as a "neurotransmitter" which is a fancy way to say it's basically a brain messenger. Serotonin transmits messages between nerve cells. It's often referred to as "the happy chemical."

Antidepressants: Anything that makes you less depressed. Most commonly known as an antidepressant drug used in treatment of mood disorder.

Neuromythology: Gross. This word has 58 syllables. It's not a buzzword, but it's equally important to define. Sometimes we say and believe in *myths* like unicorns or Hercules that are untrue or at least have no evidence whatsoever. And "neuro" is a Greek term that refers to the nervous system which starts in the brain. So neuromythology is a term referring to myths we believe about how our brain functions.

The number one neuromythology (neuromyth? Neuromythological story? I give up with this fancypants word) we believe in our society is that depression is *caused* by low serotonin levels.

I think everyone who has suffered from depression has believed that at one point! It's something we toss around as if it was as much a scientifically proven fact as water being made up of H20 molecules. Unfortunately though, it's not that simple.

In his book *Lost Connections* Johann Hari—a researcher who traveled across the world to meet with leading experts in the field of mental health to discover what really causes depression—discusses how we've been told a ridiculously simplistic version of what depression is and how to solve it. He insists that it has never been a proven fact that depression is caused by low serotonin levels. Instead, it's a myth adopted by our society because of the language pharmaceutical reps have used with us. Because of the benefit it has to their bottom line, this is what they've told us: "If your depression is purely chemical, then the solution is also purely chemical. And we have the solution for you! Simple. ______! (insert brand-name anti depression medication here)." But that is far from the truth, and it is far from that simple.

Initially when I found this out it overwhelmed me (*What do you MEAN?! I was diagnosed with clinical major depression because of a chemical imbalance! And now you're telling me that's not true?! Who even am I?! What is happening?!*), but as I dug deeper into the truth, it ended up being one of the most freeing things I'd ever learned about depression, so stick with me here.

Hari explains that believing low serotonin causes depression is like believing stretch marks cause obesity.

Oh, I was so sad when I first learned this. Why did my doctor tell me I have depression simply because of a chemical imbalance then? Was he lying? No, he wasn't outright lying at all. I likely did have a chemical imbalance, but it's inaccurate to say that the chemical imbalance came first and then caused the depression. He was just doing his job. Doing what he was trained to do. My heart was softened when I remembered that western medicine doctors are taught *medicine*—as in medication and treatments that mostly address symptoms—and that medicine is the lens they see everything through. You wouldn't go to a baker and feel upset if you told them you were hungry and all they did was give you cupcakes when what you really wanted was a chicken salad, right? If you say you are hungry, a baker will give you what they have available and what they know. If you want to have a chicken salad, you are better off finding a fresh market and not going to see a baker.

Hari discusses one of his interviews with a doctor who states that when he first began as a doctor, he felt frustrated because he was told that when patients were depressed he needed to simply tell them they had a chemical imbalance and then prescribe them a drug. But he knew the science was far more complicated than that. So he revolutionized the way he treats patients. He still occasionally prescribes traditional drugs, but it's not his immediate response.

If we shift our focus from the idea that our brains are either in or out of a constant state of "chemical balance" and instead just look at chemicals plain and simple, it might help us understand this a bit better. You know how as women we are born with all of our eggs that we'll ever have? (Awkward curveball, I know.) We know that nothing can ever change how many eggs we have in our reproductive system, and I think that's how we assume the chemicals in our brains work—almost like a fixed pie chart, with 48% happy chemicals and 52% unhappy chemicals. This is the genetic hand I've been dealt, and so that 2% imbalance makes me blue some days.

But chemicals and hormones and neurotransmitters don't work that way. They are constantly flowing, moving, balancing, re-balancing, growing, and shifting. Chemicals can be better compared to a river—always flowing, rising, falling, changing when it rains, and so on.

Let's try it right now: stop. Stop exactly where you are right now and picture an elephant.

...Do you have your elephant? Is he gray and cute and flapping his cute little ears at you?

The thought you just had right now about an elephant was due to a chemical reaction. Neurons fired and neurotransmitters and hormones and chemicals flowed, and you had a thought, like a little cloud floated over your brain-river and poured down some Dumbo.

In other words, *everything* is a chemical reaction. And yet we over-psychoanalyze and we over-spiritualize. We tend to think in categories, and we believe that the only chemical option in dealing with depression is pills. So, if I am an "all natural," hippie-dippie holistic health nut, I may not want to open a small bottle each day and swallow a pill, and if I am a by-the-books, don't-believe-anything-unless-I-heard-it-straight-from-a-doctor's-mouth believer in modern medicine, I may not want to believe there are solutions for depression besides medication.

HOWEVER. What I'm trying to say is that whether I take a pill OR do yoga as treatment for my depression, *both solutions are purely "chemical."* If I go for a run? Also chemical. If I call up my best girlfriend and have a beautiful, vulnerable ugly-crying therapy session with her? Yep. Chemical. If we simplify the science, we are all the same. ALL treatment, whether prescribed by a doctor or not, is chemical.

For those of us who fight depression without medication, we have no right to be high and mighty because we are "all natural." Rather, we are simply choosing a different route to adjust our chemicals. And for those of us who fight depression with the use of medication, we have no reason to feel guilt about it or to feel a lack of ownership over our life because every single choice, thought, or action is purely chemical.

In his book *The Noonday Demon* Dr. Andrew Solomon states that:

"If you close your eyes and think hard about polar bears (or elephants), that has a chemical effect on your brain. When you remember some episode from your past, you do so through the complex chemistry of memory. Childhood trauma and subsequent difficulty can alter brain chemistry. Thousands of chemical reactions are involved in deciding to read this book, picking it up with your hands, looking at the shapes of the letters on the page, extracting meaning from those shapes, and having intellectual and emotional responses to what they conveyed. If time lets you cycle out of the depression and feel better, the chemical changes are no less particular and complex then the ones that are brought about by taking antidepressants."

One comparison that I have often used in the past is the idea that if a diabetic needs to take insulin because of not producing enough in his pancreas, then it's the same as a depressed person who needs medication because of not producing enough serotonin. However, Solomon addresses this specifically and makes a strong case as to why this may not be a great way to approach treatment:

"Although depression is described by the popular press and the pharmaceutical industry as though it were a single effect illness such as diabetes [which means it has ONE cause—lack of an insulin-response], it is not. Indeed it is strikingly dissimilar to diabetes. Diabetics produce insufficient insulin, and diabetes is treated by increasing and stabilizing insulin in the bloodstream. Depression is not the consequence of a reduced level of anything we can now measure. Reading levels of serotonin in the brain triggers a process that eventually helps many depressed people to feel better; but that is not because they have abnormally low levels of serotonin. 'I'm depressed but it's just chemical' is a sentence equivalent to 'I'm murderous but it's just chemical' or 'I'm intelligent but it's just chemical.' Everything about a person is chemical if one wants to think in those terms. 'You can say it's 'just chemistry,' says [psychoanalyst] Maggie Robbins, who suffers from manic-depressive illness. 'I say there's nothing 'just' about chemistry.' The sun shines brightly and that's just chemical too, and it's chemical that rocks are hard, and that the sea is salt, and that certain springtime afternoons carry in their gentle breezes a quality of nostalgia that stirs the heart to longings and imaginings kept dormant by the snows of a long winter. 'This serotonin thing,' says David McDowell of Columbia University, 'is part of modern neuromythology.' It's a potent set of stories."

Okay. Deep breath. I know I just threw a lot of information at you there, but my point is that experts in the field of the mind are saying that depression is a complicated beast, *not* just a simple disease with a simple cure. Solomon says that, unlike illnesses with definitive causes or definitive starting points (such as the way one day you don't have the flu and the next day, yep, there's definitely a flu virus floating around in your bloodstream that wasn't there before) depression can better be compared to something like hunger. He writes, "Depression is like trying to come up with the clinical parameters for hunger, which affects us all several times a day, but which in its extreme version is a tragedy that kills its victims." I *love* this. Hunger is normal and healthy. Emotions are normal and healthy. But when our hunger goes untreated, it turns into starvation and can be lethal. And when our emotions dip out of the normal range and turn into depression, it can be lethal.

I should wrap these Solomon statements up by letting you know that he is quite pro-medicine as a treatment. He himself is open about his life-long prescription of antidepressants. What I love about Solomon as a psychologist though is that he is wise and humble enough to recognize that this is simply one of the treatments, not THE one and only best treatment.

I should also add that my point in bringing this up is not to sway you either way. I am not a psychiatrist by any means; I just love nerding out on research by psychologists and psychiatrists. My point is actually to empower you. We have a way of worshipping the path of least resistance. It's not that we should spend our days hustling or exhaustively fighting, it's that we should spend our days proactively *winning*.

Isn't it empowering to know that the same chemical reactions God can provide through medical intervention, *He* can also provide for you in a different form? Yeah, I said it! God has set it up in such a way that you can receive the *very same chemical reaction* simply by doing things or thinking about things that your brain associates with joy: by watching something happy, by laughing, by doing yoga, by getting some fresh air and going on a walk, by whatever.

Please hear me, sister: I am NOT saying that you can just laugh your way out of depression or that yoga is a perfect replacement for antidepressant medication. I am only trying to say that *all* of these treatments, from the pills to the yoga poses, are performing the same process chemically in your brain. We shouldn't demonize the pills, and we also shouldn't worship them. We shouldn't demonize the deep breathing or yoga poses, but we also shouldn't worship them, either.

That gets me PUMPED UP. Why would I doubt that the God I put my faith in wouldn't set me up for success in that way? God commands me to take every thought captive. He says to be transformed by the renewing of my mind. He says to meditate on His words day and night. In other words, God has been trying to get us to understand chemical reactions and mindfulness long before it was cool or "discovered" by modern science.

In modern neuroscience, we have learned through experimentation that every single thought we have is a chemical reaction. In eastern philosophy, the practice of mindfulness and meditation is one of the key tickets to happiness and peace. So, YOU GUYS, the God of the freaking Universe has been trying to tell us this for one BAJILLION years! He doesn't tell us to take every thought captive because if I think not-nice things He's going to come down on his white horse or shoot down a lightning bolt at me. Nope. He's not in the business of lightning-bolting or ought-to's. He is in the business of freedom. He has been telling us to take every thought captive because He *knows* that every thought is a chemical reaction. So we could even understand that verse as "Take every chemical reaction captive." And if we think thoughts all day long that send the stress hormone cortisol into our river of brain chemicals by the bucketload, first we're going to get TMJ or a tightness in our chest, then we'll get headaches and anxiety, and then eventually we're not going to want to leave our house or our sweatpants or our bed. I love the way the Message version of the Bible describes taking every thought captive as "using our God-tools for fitting every loose thought, emotion, and impulse into the structure of life shaped by Christ." Hooray for God's toolbox for us! A chemical toolbox is a spiritual one.

So as a coach, when I tell someone one of our main goals is to work on "positive self-talk," which is comparable to a minister saying, "What would Jesus do?", it sounds like a bumper sticker. Maybe it's something you'd roll your eyes about because you've heard it before and how could it *actually* make a difference if you are *chemically* struggling and imbalanced? And I hear things like, "Zip it, Gelly. I don't want to hear any of your positive unicorn bullcrap. I am chemically imbalanced." Well, listen here, sister: THE POSITIVE SELF-TALK *IS* CHEMICAL (I'm not yelling at you, I promise; I'm yelling WITH you), and the fact that *everything* is chemical should make you both MAD and ECSTATIC. Because Satan or The Man or whoever you want to blame has been trying to convince you that you are doomed to be depressed because of your "chemical wiring;" he wants you to believe that it is out of your hands and that God simply allowed you (or cursed you via genetics and brain chemistry) to become chemically depressed.

Well, LET'S GO AHEAD GIVE SATAN A NICE BIG KICK BETWEEN THE LEGS (This one deserved something more than just a face punch). Take your power back. God didn't give us a spirit of fear and timidity but of power, love, and self-discipline. This doesn't mean you have to sweat your way out or muscle through depression by obsessively writing happy thoughts all over your arms and forehead to have a perpetual river flow of positive chemicals (although it wouldn't hurt, haha!). It doesn't mean you have to fight this battle alone or that it's all on you. Quite the opposite, it means God gave you the tools to be well, to take back both your life, your joy, AND your chemicals. Maybe that means medicine AND other forms of antidepressants as a solution. Maybe that means non-traditional antidepressants. Whatever His story is for your *unique* healing, He's given you tools, and He's just waiting for you to pick up the toolbox.

## 45
# The Tool Box

You know how when our dads teach us to hammer a nail into a piece of wood for the first time they're right there with us, often holding the hammer or protecting our hand from being smashed? This is how I think God approaches the toolbox. He isn't asking you to pick up the toolbox and build a house by yourself. He's saying "Pick up the toolbox, and I will gently hold your hands as you hammer the first nail." Slowly, over time, as we are strengthened by God and we begin growing accustomed to hammering nails into wood, we have built an entirely new house from the foundation up.

Once more, because I reeeeeaaally want this to sink in: what are the tools of the toolbox? They are human beings who you allow to see your face, touch your hands, and make you a snack, even on the days you feel the ugliest or the lowest. They are medication. They are movement. They are deep breaths. They are laughter. They are love. They are scripture that covers us like a shield from negative thoughts and chemicals. They are moments in a day. They are chemicals, each and every one of them. Those same chemicals you studied in grade school? The ones that made you almost fail your seventh grade science class (No? Just me? Have mercy.). GOD MADE THOSE. And He wants us to use those chemicals for our healing and for His glory.

We listen better when someone whispers than when they yell, so I'm gonna whisper this bad boy (once again, a gem from the good Doctor Solomon) because I hope it echoes down into your bones and in hearing it those tired bones hold you up a little taller.

> *Listen to the people who love you. Believe that they are worth living for even when you don't believe it. Seek out the memories depression takes away and project them into the future. Be brave; be strong; take your pills. Exercise because it's good for you even if every step weighs 1000 pounds. Eat even when food itself disgusts you. Reason with yourself when you have lost your reason. These fortune cookie admonitions sound pat, but the surest way out of depression is to dislike it and not to let yourself grow accustomed to it. Block out the terrible thoughts that invade your mind.*

Embrace those chemicals of all shapes and sizes, whether they are as tiny as a pill you swallow in faith or as gigantic as a mountaintop you sit on to breathe fresh air and take in creation. Embrace all the chemicals for God's glory and for your freedom.

VITAL NOTE: please hear me here. If you are on

medication as you read this, DO NOT stop taking it. First of all, that is never, ever, ever, ever, *ever* something you should do without talking to your doctor about it first. I am not a licensed psychiatrist. I am just a girl with a humble bachelor's degree in mental health and a whole lot of depression that colored most of my days gray until I got really sick of living that way and started researching and asking questions. God's story for my healing was to eventually come off of medication, slowly, over a long period of time, and with a well-established game plan. But that doesn't mean it is His story for you. What I know is that God has a unique story with unique healing designed for you. And it may not look like mine, but it's going to be beautiful and exactly what you need.

He may not take your depression away in the exact way you'd hope, but He *will* take your hope in Him and make your shattered, tired pieces whole again.

## 46
# Like, Subscribe, Post

Some people don't need to have strict boundaries with their phone and social media. I AM NOT ONE OF THOSE PEOPLE.

You know those crazy stats that talk about the 736 times that the average person opens up Instagram or Facebook on their phone in a single day? I am pretty sure those stats are actually *just tracking me*. I'm wired for addiction, and my apps are wired to addict people like me to them. It's just the way the freaking cyber-world-cookie crumbles.

I open an app, close it, and before realizing what I'm even doing, I'm opening the same app I just closed 45 seconds ago. *Listen Gelly, NOTHING* that *awesome happened in those forty five seconds. Oprah did not slide into your DM's. You didn't go viral. You didn't win that big giveaway that the cute mom hosted giving away 4,000 dollars worth of organic baby food and butt wipes. And even if those things* did *happen by some miracle, the world will not end and those opportunities won't vanish if you wait an entire five tortuous minutes before opening it up again, for crying out loud. Compose yourself, woman!*

Addictions feel so icky because you have this overwhelming loss of control. You know you shouldn't click the thing or drink the thing or engage in the activity, but it feels like you can't help it. This is why the boundaries and parameters I set (and am trying to set) don't *limit me*, they actually *free me*. It is precisely 0% fun to feel out of control and enslaved to something.

So, here are the parameters I am setting when it comes to the pocket-sized access to the universe we carry around. I do my best here you guys; I don't do this perfectly.

First of all, my phone is almost always on silent. This boundary drives some of my people up a wall because I rarely answer the phone right away. There are exceptions, of course—when I'm waiting for an important call, my husband is traveling, or my daughter is with a babysitter—but otherwise, I let go of my reigns on the *entire earth* and remind myself that if I am not immediately alerted with a notification about everything under the sun, the world will keep spinning. I check the phone on *my terms*, not on the world's and all of its zillions of push-notifications.

Secondly, I sleep with my phone in the kitchen. Not every night, but most nights. It's a whopping 30 feet from the bedroom to the kitchen, but when I'm out of the habit, it feels like a hundred miles away from civilization. I have to remind myself that for literally, oh you know, EVER, we not only survived but *flourished* as a human race without access to the planet sitting next to our heads while we slept. I think to myself, *What if there's a fire? What if a family member needs me? What if we are robbed in the middle of the night and the fact that I have to walk to the kitchen to get my phone to call 911 is the reason I am shot?* These are all valid points. But I think there are other ways to prepare for worst-case-scenarios that don't include basing my life decisions out of fear of what-if's. Living in fear is no way to live.

Third, I don't bring my phone into the bathroom anymore. I bring a book. Or I sit and meditate. Can you believe human beings used to go number one AND number two without their phones in their hands? I mean, it's barbaric really.

My husband will read this and say, "YOU FILTHY LIAR. You brought your phone into the bathroom with you just this morning!" To which I can only say, "Yeah. You're right." Sometimes I forget. I slip up. I do the things I don't want to do when I'm on autopilot. But the more I practice doing everything mindfully (yep, even mindfully using the potty), the more I am finding freedom.

Lastly, I try to remember that *I am what I do daily.* Social media is *not* something I personally want on the list of things that define who I am because it's a part of my everyday life. So on Tuesdays and Thursdays I hide the apps that tempt me most in an inconvenient folder, and I don't check them all day. As an "influencer," that's social media suicide. All the head honchos say posting daily is a *must* in order to stay fresh on people's feeds. But I don't want you to need to hear from me daily in order to live a good life. I want you to live a good life regardless of me. I want you to live a good life because *you are worth living a good life*, not because I post daily with just the right words to get you up and going. So I excuse myself from the pressure to post daily because I don't want you to need me daily. Plus, get serious. It's *two days* out of seven. That's still a lot of days on social media, my friends. That's still a lot of Gelly in your face and a lot of media consumption for *me*. And I think it's quite enough.

There's so much grace with this, too. Maybe one week I have a particular piece of content I'm posting that needs more of my engagement online. Maybe that week I only take one day off from the socials. Other weeks, maybe it's slow and quiet and I give myself an entire week break. Maybe there are entire seasons where I just need the apps deleted from my phone altogether—I did this over Christmas this last season, and I was off of social media entirely for about 4-5 weeks. And it was so refreshing. There's no perfect equation here. The idea is just that I am intentional about not getting on daily because what I do daily defines me.

47

# Clutter

You might be thinking I'm jumping on the Marie Kondo train and I'm about to tell you to hold your belongings against your heart and see what sparks joy (and if you have no idea what I'm talking about, Kondo is all the rage right now in the minimalism world). But the reality is I've been addicted to all sorts of stuff—actual physical stuff, as in crap in my house—long before Marie's Netflix debut.

When Ricky and I first got married, our tiny one bedroom apartment had so many knick-knacks, piles of random trinkets, and pieces of different colored furniture that it looked like a hybrid of a Mexican restaurant and your neighbor's garage sale. I was always getting more stuff, even if it was just from thrift stores, and I was never willing to get rid of anything. The things I kept that I didn't need always fell under one of two categories: my what-if-one-day's and my sentimental value items. Look, I'm all for sentimental objects, but the problem is that I am *overly* sentimental. Sometimes you just have to draw the line. I will probably survive just fine if I get rid of that disintegrating napkin with the note written on it that my husband passed to me in class one time while we were still dating. The rock I nervously played with in my hand while we went on our first long walk together? Girl, just let it go back home to its family. Everything will be fine. What if instead of keeping all the unnecessary momentos, you kept your husband in your heart all day so that when he comes home from work he can't help but notice how delighted you are to see him? (Not to mention it's easier to feel delighted when you didn't just spend an entire day reorganizing the piles of crap that are just going to get messed up again tomorrow anyway.)

I always assumed the problem was that we needed more closets, more storage, more space. I've gone through two or three (or seven or eight) seasons of life where I spend far too much time on Zillow looking for bigger houses to fit all our stuff, but have you ever noticed that it really doesn't matter how much bigger your next home is? It still ends up just as cluttered.

I think what we actually want is *free* space, but what we *think* we want is *more* space. We think having more space will give us more free space, but if we never handle our habit/addiction of more-stuff-always, it doesn't matter how much more space we get. We'll always fill it up with more stuff.

I operate similarly when it comes to time. I pack my days so full with endless piles of appointments and to-do lists that I find myself constantly driving around as if I was late. I'm in a perpetual rush to get to the next thing, and

I'm constantly wishing for more time.

But what if my schedule, just like my house, needs free time instead of more time—free time where I can stop to talk to people as I run into them instead of zip through and wave from afar because I've got a thing to get to? Free time where I can breathe slowly and fully enjoy the moment without the next event or deadline or appointment hanging over my head?

All the clutter—whether in my home, my schedule, or my heart—just gets to me. It chips away at my spirit until I feel buried in it all and can hardly recognize myself or the people I love. When I start feeling that anxiety in my chest, I know I've got some clutter to clear out. It's so hard though, isn't it? I see the deals on cute clothes or home decor and I want them...over and over again. I'm approached with opportunities, and I want to say yes...over and over again. I want to be involved. I want to have a cute, modern house with all the mid-century-with-a-boho-latin-twist decor. But all of that exhausting chasing weighs me down because I'm never content with what I have or fully present in the moment. It's like going through my life only half-alive because part of me is always somewhere else or wanting something else.

I'm growing to accept my need for simplicity and slowing one day at a time. I need slowness in my life the same way I need air. I don't realize I haven't been taking life in fully until I start taking shallow breaths. All of a sudden I'm needing to slow *myself* down and my *breath* down. And I'm learning to be okay with having a lower capacity than some people when it comes to how much I can fit in my schedule, or how much stuff I'm able to keep tidy and maintain in my home compared to others. I'm okay with not being *superwoman* because it gives me *superpeace* (yeah...that sounded cooler in my head). I'm more than okay with not being the best if it means I'm doing my best, if it means I'm taking fuller breaths. It's a little mantra I've been repeating to myself these days: own less, rush less, and hustle less, so I can breathe more.

## 48
# The Burning Hoo-ha and the Balloon Tongue

During our first year of marriage, I went to the doctor to ask about why I'd been getting almost monthly urinary tract infections since we got married. YES, monthly. Did I want to die? Of course. Having a UTI is like peeing knives. It's the absolute worst. Yes, I peed after sex. At one point we were showering BEFORE AND AFTER sex out of paranoia. There was no cuddling for us after making love because I would sprint to the bathroom with my gallon of cranberry juice and sit on the toilet drinking and peeing. I know, *so sexy*. You want to suck 100% of the romance and spontaneity out of sex? Get first in line for monthly UTI's when they're on sale at the local hate-your-life market. That oughta do the trick.

So, if you know anything about traditional treatments for infections like that, you're already assuming I was also on antibiotics about once a month, and you are correct. You guys, I won't get into gut health quite yet, but being on antibiotics once a month is like personally hiring a SWAT team to climb inside of your stomach and destroy you. All of you. The infection AND anything healthy. No survivors. This is not a good thing. You need healthy bacteria in your gut to stay alive.

I was never allowed to donate blood in high school because every time they'd do a quick check of my levels I was way too iron-deficient to donate blood.

I ALSO had a horrible case of eczema—on my FACE of all places—on top of already having rosacea. Oy vey.

Ready for one more thing?

Since I was little, my tongue would randomly swell into a big angry balloon with white slashes down the sides. Yeah, sounds cute, right? It was incredibly painful. This was not an STD (although my six year-old self who'd only ever made out with my own hand after watching Spanish soap operas felt allllll the shame that comes with a real STD diagnosis).

Now, are you asking yourself, "Gelly, why the heck are you telling us all of your gross physical ailments?" Stay with me! I swear I'm going somewhere with all this! Let's jump to adulthood. I am 24, well into our second year of marriage. I've put on a significant amount of weight. My tongue still randomly swells up like a balloon, I've been on anti-depression meds for about four years now. And I'm exhausted 100% of the time. I still can't donate blood. My face is bumpy, itchy, and almost always red. And I start regularly having crazy stomach pain that leaves me hunched over like I'm going into labor every time it hits.

I finally go to our new family doctor who is as holistic in knowledge as traditional doctors come, and here's what he tells me in my follow up appointment after the blood work. Even on hypo-anemia medication (the kind they give to women who are having fertility issues), I was still incredibly low in iron which, he explained to me, indicated that my problem wasn't the amount of iron I was taking in but rather how much my body could absorb (ummm, what? Come again?). In other words, it didn't matter how much iron I took in, my body wasn't processing and retaining it correctly.

So, Doc, what you're telling me is I'm doomed? Yes? Perfect.

As for my chronic UTI's? "Some people are just prone to them." Great, more doom.

The depression? "Low serotonin. Some people are just low." Doomed forever.

Red skin and eczema? You guessed it, doomed.

And then he off-handedly dropped this somewhat (re: extremely) contradictory bomb on me kind of under his breath: "You could probably fix a lot of these things by seeing a nutritionist, but who has time for that?"

Cue loud record scratch—*Um, excuse me, BRO, what did you just say to me?*

I sort of went into shock and couldn't think of anything to say. The depression, the burning hoo-ha, the anemic exhaustion, the balloon tongue, the eczema, the stomach aches… I was doomed to suffer them forever, but also they could all be fixed through nutrition? I had nothing to say. I was too angry.

Even though I was furious at the time, those were the most important words that any doctor has ever said to me.

Those words sent me down a rabbit trail. A hunt. In my head I went full on Amazon warrior, complete with spear and loincloth (and maybe topless? I had no time to put on a leaf and twigs bra if I had 'no time to contact a nutritionist', *duh*). I researched. Read. Experimented.

I took my health into my own hands when I wasn't satisfied with the diagnosis I was given.

And now, I am going on five years FREE of depression meds, free of a single UTI, free of the balloon tongue, free of face rashes, and walking around with healthy blood levels without any supplementation whatsoever.

My addiction to food was slowly wrecking my body. I was diagnosed with ulcerative colitis (it's just as gross as it sounds), and whether or not it was partially due to being genetically predisposed to it or entirely due to how I'd been eating my whole life didn't matter. The point was that my body needed restoration. I'm still on the healing journey, actually, and when I cave into my strong addictions to some foods that make my body go insane, I'm reminded of how addicted I truly am. What hole am I trying to fill in those moments when I'm emotionally eating? How is it that I can know my body will react so violently, and yet I'm willing to eat the thing anyway? That right there is addiction, my friends.

Like pretty much everything else in my life, I don't do nutrition perfectly. It's a growing process, but it has drastically improved. I've gone years without a relapse and then had seasons where I am unloving to my body with my choices. It's not a perfect linear progression, but it's an upward spiral. Embracing that kind of progress is the most loving thing I can do.

Maybe you're bored because none of this pertains to you, but please let me just say one more thing: my body used these symptoms to cry out. It was how my body uniquely expressed that there were some underlying issues that needed to be addressed.

We all have different physiological wiring, so our bodies express stress differently, even if they have the same underlying issue that I have. So maybe your hoo-ha hasn't burned a day in your life and your tongue is always as sleek and slender as they come, but maybe you have experienced chronic headaches or fatigue? Anxiety? Joint soreness or pain? Brain fog? Mood swings? The list goes on and on. Just because you don't get a stomach ache when you eat things doesn't mean your body isn't trying to tell you something in a different way.

Food itself, even if we're struggling with our weight, can actually keep us small: the kind of small that makes us live a lifetime of disease, suffering, or just not being our truest selves.

## 49
# Comfortable Confessions

You know those people who leave their underwear on the floor *just to the right* of the laundry basket instead of walking the extra half a foot to put it directly *in* the basket? Or those people who always leave their plate out after dinner so that the food gets cemented on and takes three times as long to scrub? Yes? No? Well, what about the guy who will ask you to grab him something from the kitchen even though you *just finally sat down* and he's actually sitting *closer* to the kitchen than you are?

No? Not ringing a bell yet? Okay, what if we trace our memory back a little further: maybe it was the guy in gym class who always sat around complaining about how horrible it was that he was being asked to exert any physical energy whatsoever?

Oh. Well, unless you were in the Bobcats class of '08, maybe you wouldn't know.

Because, well, it was me. I was always *that guy.*

I know. Curveball. You probably thought I was ragging on someone else, didn't you? Nope. Guilty as charged.

In every single way, and on every single day, I based most of my decisions—big or small—on whether or not I would have to get uncomfortable. Whether it was a stroll around the gymnasium or a stroll from the couch to the kitchen, if it meant getting uncomfortable, well, *no gracias.* I would run for the hills.

For example, there's this thing that happens to your muscles when you're working out called "lactic acid buildup." Commonly known as "feeling the burn." It's that sensation you get in your thighs when you're running or squatting that kind of makes it feel like they're ON FIRE. Well, lactic acid buildup hurts, but over time you can increase your tolerance to it, and your muscles get better at handling it (i.e., you get stronger). But the teenage me wouldn't know because the few times I tried to work out when I was younger, the moment I felt that burning sensation… LORD-JESUS-SEND-YOUR-ANGELS...I was DONE. I quit.

I was always quitting everything when it got hard.

I remember the moment that I pushed past that pain for the first time. You guys, you're going to laugh at me, but I CRIED while doing squats holding one small dumbbell.

In the middle of the gym, with all the beefcakes and athletic girls watching, I *cried actual tears.* And it wasn't a super strenuous workout, either. I just had never before finished the number of reps I was planning on doing because I'd always quit when it started to hurt. My husband was there being his faithful-cheerleader-self and encouraging me, "You can do it, babe!!" And we caused one heck of a scene. But I finished every rep on my piece of paper for the FIRST TIME EVER. In my mind, it was a Rocky-movie-montage-moment with music playing in the background. In everyone else's mind, I was the weird girl in uncool work out clothes that clearly didn't know what she was doing and was also awkwardly crying.

But I didn't die. I felt a little bit of discomfort, and I didn't die from it. And that moment was a game changer for me.

Seven years later (well, last week actually) I had a close friend tell me my new haircut was *fine* but that it was also just "safe." Oh yeah, and she *knew* what she was doing when she said it. I looked her square in the eyes and said, "Oh yeah?" And then immediately went out and got an asymmetrical pixie cut. Sliced off 15 inches just like that. Because hair is hair, and it will grow back. But purposefully putting myself out of my comfort zone? Well, that's a discipline—it's a discipline that's helped to set me free to be who I am today because all the years of staying safe and comfortable kept me small and scared. It doesn't matter if I'm challenging myself to be brave with my haircut, my career, or my workout plan—getting outside of my comfort zone frees me.

I lived so many years addicted to comfort that now I make a lot of decisions in direct opposition to it. Only to a certain degree, of course: I have yet to feel the need to go skydiving or swim with sharks. It's not about being a daredevil just for the sake of adrenaline or to torture myself. But if I'm avoiding something solely out of fear, insecurity, or wanting to stay safe and comfortable...*especially* when deep down I *want* to try, but I'm just scared or being lazy? Well, then I'm chasing that thing head on RIGHT FRIGGIN' NOW. It's the reason I work out. It's the reason I trained for a half-marathon. It's the reason I'll cut all my hair off without worrying too much about it. It's the reason I'll get up and speak in front of people even though I feel so nervous I might puke. It's the reason I make my bed every single morning. Because, by default, I'm the guy that leaves clothes on the floor, never makes the bed, and never tries anything hard. And I don't want to be that guy anymore.

What about you? Am I alone here?

Have you ever avoided something you wanted to try out of fear? Or quit a workout early because it started to hurt a little?

Don't get me wrong here, friends. I am such an advocate for listening to our bodies. It's not about torturing ourselves or ignoring healthy limits. But I *do* think there's value in recognizing the areas we might be staying safe or sluggish in if that is not actually good for us. My comfort is rarely the catalyst for a good life; just a safe one. But I've found the most joy and fulfillment in my life in the moments when I'm brave.

Just ask my husband. Life is so much better for everyone involved when I *courageously* put my clothes in the laundry basket instead of *safely* on the floor. Ha!

## 50
# The Way Things Should Be

I woke up one cold, gray Sunday morning with an inexplicable queasiness in my bones.

*"My family is about to implode,"* I heard those same queasy bones whisper into my blood until the words circulated enough times from my toes to my ears that I not only heard it but believed it.

I didn't know what it meant or exactly who it was referring to, I just knew it was true.

I got ready and went to church like I usually do, trying to ignore the uneasiness, and I remember that as I walked into the building it felt like I was watching my body in slow motion from a distance. As I watched from outside myself, I was uninterested in socializing because I could hardly hear anything above the thuds coming from behind my chest. It's the way hearts beat when they're bracing for impact, and it would have made holding any real conversation difficult.

I stayed towards the back of the church because I felt like a ticking time bomb, unsure of when the whisper in me might surface into some kind of exploding emotion. The music started and the congregation stood firmly on their legs. Their eyes turned to read lyrics on the screen.

My legs, however, collapsed beneath me and my eyes flooded with salt and water as I read the words:

*Your love's not fractured*
*It's not a troubled mind*
*It isn't anxious*
*It's not the restless kind*
*Your love's not passive*
*It's never disengaged*
*It's always present*
*It hangs on every word we say*
*Love keeps it promises*
*It keeps its word*
*It honors what's sacred*
*Cause its vows are good*
*Your love's not broken*
*It's not insecure*
*Your love's not selfish*
*You love is pure..."*

It felt like ten years of counseling and discovery had rushed into my body in a matter of minutes. I was sick to my stomach because a love I'd known for 16 years was slipping from between my fingers. To this day I still don't understand it, but somehow I knew divorce was about to hit my family again. I learned later that day that God had given me the exact words I needed in order to soften the blow. Just an hour after church, my dad asked to get coffee with me and informed me that he and my stepmother of 16 years were separating.

My dad, who did not want to tell me this awful news near the end of my pregnancy just weeks before my daughter was born, was completely caught off guard by how at peace I was with the decision. Although I was sad that our family would experience loss through this decision, I had known for a long time that there were deep-seated issues making the marriage toxic for both people and that perhaps they'd be healthier apart. It wasn't the loss through their ending things that rattled me, it was that there was an ending at all.

What saved me that day was those lyrics, read through teary eyes on an average Sunday morning at church. When I felt all my pieces shattered on the ground, each piece another broken promise, the truth about God's love slowly picked me up off the floor and put me back together.

This Love. The One that isn't fragile the way my body was as I fell to pieces sitting in the back of the church.

This Love. The One that keeps its promises unlike everyone around me since I was little.

I spent the first half of that hour-long church service shattered, mourning, and collapsing bit by bit as the reality of another divorce—which, might I remind you, was still just technically a hunch, not a confirmed fact—came crashing down on me. The tears were heavy. I was mourning the put-together family I'd always wanted. I was letting go of my expectations, detoxing, even, from my addiction to control, to wanting everything to be as it should.

But doesn't detoxing always feel so good after the initial shock? The second half of that service held some of the most surreal and peaceful minutes of my life. I felt hands gently picking me up off the floor, slowly stitching all my shattered pieces back together. I heard another whisper, and this time it didn't come from my bones:

"As the promises of this life bend and and twist and break, *My* promise to you never changes."

I looked up at the screen and read those lyrics again.

> *Your love's not broken*
> *It's not insecure*
> *Your love's not selfish*
> *You love is pure.*

Those words were the reason that, though I started the day feeling inexplicable pain, a few hours later I was resting in inexplicable peace. If I hadn't gone through the breaking and the putting back together that morning and felt the confidence and assurance of God's never-changing love regardless of the many endings we face on a regular basis in this life, I probably would not have responded so well.

I didn't want to face the fact that my daughter, who would be born in less than fourteen days, would be born into a world where no promises are ever kept, where she would not know what it was like to have a grandpa and grandma love each other until death do they part.

I went through a few weeks of the same cycle I experienced that morning—the breaking and the repairing, the fear and the reassurance. I finally felt like it was affecting me enough that I was seeing red flags: I felt paralyzed by my wrestling with the sadness one day and swallowed up entirely by my anxiety the next, so I contacted our friend and counselor Steve. He agreed to meet with Ricky and I to help bring me some peace and figure out what all I was feeling.

Let me tell you about Steve. Have you ever heard of the spiritual gift of "*soul x-ray vision?*" Well, he's got it. Steve is the kind of person who can hear you speak for no less than 15 seconds before he already has a keen insight into the condition of your soul and the root of the problem. After hearing me speak for probably far longer than necessary, he asked me a question that both pierced me deeply and relieved me:

"Are you wanting your daughter to be born into

Eden?"

Without skipping a beat I buried my face in my palms and began crying. He had apparently hit a nerve. My soul knew it. He knew it. My hands knew it as they cradled my face. But I did not fully know it.

I finally gained some composure and peeked one eye through my hands. He knew I needed him to explain why on earth that had hit such a button, and so he continued with something that went like this:

"The weight of the fact that your daughter is being born into a broken world is crashing down on you. Your maternal instincts want to protect her, want her to be born into Eden, of course. This is where we are designed to live, so of course you want that for her. But we simply can't have it on this side of heaven. Let go of how you think things ought to be. *She needs a mother with Eden in her heart.* This is your peace as you welcome your daughter: being a mother to her with Eden in your heart. This is the best gift you can give your daughter."

When things are not all that they should be, when my addiction to control and peace and the perfect family is met by the cold, hard reality of my actual circumstances, I am so grateful to have experienced a peace and a Love that is so unshakeable that I am able to capture some of it (or rather be captured by it) and keep it in my heart. This was not the first time nor would it be the last that I had to wrestle with my addiction to how I thought the world should be, but I have so much joy now knowing that my well-being rests in the hands of a God who loves me with a love more powerful than anything else I could find this side of Eden.

**Strip Off: Addiction**

Whether big or small, addictions shrink us, control us, and imprison us.

**Step Into: Something You Can Dance In**

The prize that comes from stepping out of prisons is freedom. True freedom. It's the way my daughter twirls around in our living room during her favorite songs. She's weightless. She's captivated. She's full of joy and light-hearted. She's free.

**GV Fashion Tip**

What if you wear something today that you can dance freely in? Something in which you can dip, twist, and shake however you want. Go out of your way to dance today. Why wear something if you can't dance in it, anyway?

*If I can't dance in it I don't want to wear it.*

# GUNK COVERING GOLD

51
# Hiding

I want you to know that my husband is one of the pastors at my church. Which is only significant in this story because right now as we speak, I am *skipping* church. Yep, you heard me...playing hooky. Holy hooky. If that's not a model pastor's wife, I don't know what is.

The thing is, tomorrow morning the first draft of the book you now hold in your hands is due. My Saint of a friend Libby (who basically has her PhD in cheerleader-ing) texted me yesterday saying "I'll be at your house at 8:30 AM to pick up your daughter so you can finish this project."

You see, Libby is a planner. I, on the other hand, am one of those "God will make a way!" kind of planners... which *really* means that I have no plan whatsoever. I am basically hoping time magically appears in my schedule. Sometimes it does. Other times (most times), it doesn't and I fall very, *very* behind. I responded to her in all caps saying, "I WILL HAVE CHURCH WITH JESUS AND MY LAPTOP," to which she responded, "THAT IS EXACTLY WHAT NEEDS TO HAPPEN."

The important part though is not me justifying my need to skip church because free babysitting is hard to come by (feel free to agree or disagree; it's a free country). The important part is actually what happened next.

I started typing out a text for my husband that said, "If people ask where I am, do NOT tell them I'm working on my book!" I didn't care what he said instead, "She has explosive diarrhea" or "She's having a mental health day and staying home to watch Netflix" or "She just plain didn't feel like coming today." I didn't care what the excuse was so long as it wasn't the *truth*.

I didn't want him to tell the truth, and not because I thought working on a book deadline wasn't a good enough reason to skip church (especially as the pastor's wife, hello!). I didn't want him to tell the truth because I am totally embarassed to admit to some people that I am writing a book, and it was too risky not knowing who might ask him where I was if I couldn't control the response. When some people write or sing or do basically anything at all, they announce their projects from the rooftops. I, however, whisper them to a few select safe people and hope that word doesn't travel far.

Oftentimes when someone asks me about my writing, I shrivel up. I get small and I make it small: "Oh it's whatever, just a little project I'm working on for fun." But that is a dirty filthy lie. There I go again. I would rather stay safe than tell the truth because standing up tall, smiling, and speaking proudly about myself and these written words might come off as *vain*, or it might be scary, or I might get rejected or feel stupid. But when I shrivel up instead of standing up when I talk about this book, I am not being honest because this book is not just *whatever.* This book is the key that the God of the Freaking Universe is using to bring me out of so many of my prisons. It's the knife that is cutting through the tightly wound strings of a corset I've been wearing that is made up of standards, fears, and expectations that have been cutting off my air supply for almost 29 years.

So here I am, working on literally the last section of the book, and I inserted this little part on the last day because *I just almost did it again.* I almost stayed small. I almost sent that text. But then I erased it. I said to myself, *No, I won't micromanage conversations because of my fear. Let them ask what they want to ask. And then let my husband, with pride that his wife is hustling to finish a* huge *project that has been a* lifelong DREAM, *respond in whatever big way he wants to.*

This is the hiding we do. We have felt belittled our entire lives, and so we jump on the bandwagon and belittle ourselves, our dreams, and the gold buried inside of us. The hardest part, however, is that it's not just as simple as letting the gold come out, is it? I think that like most of us,

I didn't even realize there was any gold in me at all because of all the layers of gunk covering it up.

## 52
# The Build Up

I grew up with a pen and journal attached to my hip. Words, characters, stories, and melodies filled me up and spilled out onto the paper daily. That is, until I was 8 years old, and the journal I kept under my pillow was replaced by a calendar with one sole purpose: I used it to mark a big red X over the days that my parents' fights got so loud I had to hide in my room with a pillow over my ears. As the red on the calendar began bleeding over entire months, the words and stories in my soul got quieter and quieter until they were finally silenced altogether.

Trauma, depression, anxiety, insecurities; these things have a way of suppressing who we were made to be. And I don't think it's that we become any less incredible, it's that all our gifts and passions just get stuffed, suppressed, and backed up.

The author Anne Lamott describes writers as engorged cows needing to be milked (how's that for a visual?). When cows don't get milked they are uncomfortable, weighed down, and likely even in pain. And as people full of passions and callings, we are the same. When we don't vulnerably create and empty ourselves of what's been put inside of us to share, we feel heavy, uncomfortable, and likely in some degree of physical or emotional pain.

We don't create out of some narcissistic desire to have people read, hear, or see what we have to say (although, of course, when our creative work *does* find an audience, we both love and hate it—we love feeling heard, yet are terrified of putting our heart out there on display for others to dissect or critique.). No, we create because we can't NOT create. Because if we don't live out our calling, we are heavy. We are uncomfortable. And it's often not until after we've tried that we feel the weight lifted. You don't know how weighed down you actually are until you feel the relief as the weight lifts once you start trying. There is something in you that needs to come out into the light, and when it does the pieces of your soul that feel stuck in shadows will slowly start to feel the light too.

If depression suppressed our dreams, let's use our dreams to suppress our depression.

It will feel uninspiring at first. You will doubt your abilities and your calling. But do it anyway. There is a theory in writing that says it's necessary to start every morning by writing "morning pages." It's the first things that come out of us—the yucky, stale water stuck in the tap that we have to pump out before the clear flowing streams flow out to refresh—that are often the gunk covering up our gold. So whether it's writing, painting, music or flippin' *geometry*—if it's been a while, you have some built up gunk to get out. Stick with it though. The gold inside you is so worth it. Sit down and write. Paint. Sing. Do the math problem. Go to a quiet room, and get alone with your soul, and let it bring forth both the gunk and the gold that is screaming to be let out.

## 53
# Intimacy and Intelligent Design

I don't know what you believe in that is bigger than you. Maybe it's the sun. Maybe it's the little god inside of each human. Maybe it's the universe. Maybe it's the God of the universe. Maybe it's the goodness we all carry somewhere inside us as a human race. And *maybe* where you're at in life right now the only thing you can muster up belief in is the goodness of the plate of loaded nachos you destroyed last night or the goodness of a Taco Bell run at 3 AM (oh, I've BEEN THERE, my friend; I'd be lying if I said I didn't have seasons where the only thing I confidently put my faith in was my ability to sink my teeth into a Crunch Wrap Supreme). Regardless, it's safe to admit that *something* bigger than both of us may very well exist.

I heard a theory once arguing for intelligent design that went something like this:

Assuming that after the Big Bang all of the elements and energy and stardust and chemical and physical reactions and physical *stuff* of the universe swirled around and magically came together to form planets and stars and solar systems and galaxies and then, miraculously, our own perfect little green and blue world just "poofed" together one day in some cosmic explosion is so preposterous, so *profoundly* unlikely, that to believe in it would be like assuming that if you were to throw eggs, sugar, flour, butter, and baking soda in a tornado and wait a few million years, eventually a perfectly baked cake would pop out all on its own.

I thought that was pretty cool.

Regardless, let's assume there was at least *some* degree of intentionality when the molecules that make you *you* were formed together. Let's even assume *you* happened on purpose. And with that purpose, you were carefully and uniquely crafted like a road map that leads to unique places, people, and treasures.

I believe God put treasures in you and when you hunt for them it's self-discovery. Self-discovery in and of itself is a form of worship for whomever or whatever it is that made you. Finding your hidden jewels is a spiritual experience because it's intimacy with the Creator of the Universe. The very act of making art requires reflection—about the self, about the world, about something. It is really hard to reflect about anything without experiencing some degree of self-discovery. And I think that's why being a creative person is so life-giving. Creating something means you are connecting to someone, whether it's yourself, someone else, or something bigger than you. It's connection. Connection to self. Connection to others.

Connection to God. It's why digging deep into who we are and what we love matters. It isn't selfish to do what you love. It's worship.

And honestly, that self-discovery-adventure-of-communing-with-something-bigger-than-me-worship is what I need to make good art, regardless of what my craft may be. Because I am convinced that the secret ingredient to good art is not its shape, color, sound, or even its profitability, but rather its reckless, love-blinded unwillingness to apologize for who or what it is.

I think it's the deeper meaning behind telling someone to "Just own it." I don't know if you've seen the runways at fancy fashion shows these days with the body suits that look like Godzilla took a poop on a Christmas tree and then set it on fire or the girl strutting like a friggin' Queen while wearing a bubble dress resembling the nerdy kid from the Sandlot (all you have to do is google "fashion runway" images to find the exact outfits I'm describing; it's literally the tab open next to this page on my computer). But when it comes to clothes, you can rock pretty much anything and call it fashion as long as you *own it* with all your heart.

Think about the people who have pushed our boundaries and how we have responded by calling them legendary geniuses.

Frida Kahlo, for example, was a Mexican artist from the early 1900's whose signature move was the unibrow (again, another opportunity to utilize Google. Go ahead. I'll wait. It's so worth it.). And she rocked that unibrow *hard.* It didn't matter if it was generally frowned upon for humans to have one single eyebrow instead of two. She decided that she loved hers and that she was going to make it freaking art and that you were going to love it.

As consumers, I don't think we love art when it's "good." I don't even think we are left in awe when art is *perfect*. Honestly, I think we *adore* art when it bears the soul of a human unapologetically. We *adore* art when it's brave, not when it's flawless. We are drawn to vulnerability, even if we don't realize that it's that vulnerability that is pulling us in. Have you ever noticed how seeing a musician play live is way more exciting—even when they mess up or don't sing perfectly on pitch—than when their vocals and instruments have been scrubbed clean in the studio? Their raw, brave, vulnerable art is what draws us in.

We are inexplicably drawn to *soul art*: the kind of art that knows that in showing its face, it frees a soul, heals a wound, and raises oceans within us. It's the reason some melodies make me cry, and I can't explain why. It's the reason we can each probably think of at least one or two books off the top of our head that have changed our lives. It's the reason some paintings depict the color of our heartache or joy better than words ever could. This is especially true when *we* are the one making the soul art. Oh man. That "ocean-rising" line is no joke. It feels like a hurricane inside you when you first start creating. And I can imagine that each project brings a new internal storm, too, because being vulnerable hurts a little (or a lot.). But when the freaking ocean rises and the hurricane spins everything around for a while and then finally begins to settle, it uncovers Atlantis—the lost city within each of us—paved with gold.

Let the hurricane rise, dear one. The infinite gold in you is worth the temporary storm.

## 54
# Practice Makes ~~Perfect~~

So now what?

What do we do with that? We know there's gold in us, or at least we want to believe there is, but it's still terrifying to actually start digging for it.

I started my digging process by slowly unfolding this truth: as a human race, we actually have very little interest in perfection. Even though it seems to be the standard we all drive ourselves bonkers trying to achieve, no one else actually cares about me and my perfection or you and your perfection. (I should add a cliffs note here that *sometimes* the unhealthy people in our lives *do* appear to expect perfection from us...in which case I would simply remind you of two things: 1. if they expect that, well, they aren't healthy themselves, and it's probably a good idea not to put too much stock in what unhealthy people have to say about your life unless you too want your life to be unhealthy, and 2. I'll direct you to the first section of this book again: strip off their opinions, sister. Strip them off with the same urgency you'd strip off a sweater made of sandpaper!)

Practice doesn't make perfect, and I'd argue that we don't even *want* it to make perfect. Practice makes *peace.*

Practice says, "I am a human living in a world with uncontrollable variables like weather, other people, unforeseeable circumstances, and so on, and therefore, I cannot possibly do a *damn* thing perfectly. But I did my part in practicing, so I'm at peace with the outcome regardless of what happens." So *why not try*? If perfection is no longer a goal, what do you have to lose? Why not just give the gold in you a chance?

Furthermore, I think it's the act of practice itself that gives us peace. Practice, or the process, is the most rewarding part of it all. When this book is finished, it won't be the hard copy I hold in my hands that has changed me or freed me. It will be the hours I spent wrestling with myself and dancing with God, playing with words, and experimenting in truth-telling (no matter how much it scared me) that changed me and freed me.

Practice makes peace, not perfection.

# 55
# Buried Gold

I have such a hard time understanding people without dreams. And while at first I thought it was a creatives thing, I realized over time that it's less about being right-brained or left-brained and more about being a creator because creators are growing, evolving, learning.

So when I ask a friend, "Tell me about your dreams?" I don't mean, "What did you want to be when you grew up?" I mean, "What is your heart excited about? What's been growing you? What are you growing toward?" I love a Grower. And I think dreaming and growing are synonymous—dreaming just means having a vision for something more, and it's typically the result of believing that you are *worth* more.

For those who don't dream, it's not that they aren't creative enough, it's that they don't believe they are worth enough. Sister, YOU ARE WORTH ENOUGH. Dream! Create! Grow! Just start doing it, whether that means getting really excited about something as simple as a new recipe to bless your family with (and by simple, I mean "commonly perceived as ordinary," NOT easy...because Lord knows I can't even get a "simple" mac and cheese recipe right) or doing something as extraordinary as traveling to another country. It could be starting a business. It could be picking up an old hobby that used to make your soul come alive but was cast aside after work and kids and life took precedence. Whatever your dream is, see yourself as worth having it. THAT pumps me up.

Some of us, when we were younger and first got excited about growing, dreaming and making, were told, "Stop it. It's not safe" or "That's silly." And our spirits were crushed. But most of the time that kind of response comes from fear masked in love. The thought goes something like, "You shouldn't encourage your child to try that risky thing, because they might fail, and if they fail, they might hurt."

But you know what hurts more than failing? Always wondering "What if." Silencing a part of yourself in order to stay safe will shut down a human heart and produce the kind of pain that sews itself into your DNA until you forget how it feels to live a pain-free life altogether. That exhaustion you feel in your bones that makes you tired 24/7? It could be a buried dream weighing you down.

The thing is, when your soul really loves something, the beauty is not in whether or not you succeed. The beauty is in doing the thing itself. This book, for example: I wrote it for me, not for you. And while I hope you like it, I won't be constantly checking in to see if you do. I've committed to not reading a *single* review. Because I know that if I'm reading the good ones I'm doing it to give me permission to keep writing and if I'm reading the negative ones they will, by default, convince me once and for all that I should never write again and I am the worst writer to ever walk the face of the earth.

But writing this book was the most freeing thing I've ever done in my life, and that is the only review I need: the "review" of the woman's face in the mirror that smiles and speaks and sings more freely than I've ever been able to in my life.

If you are human, you have creativity in your bones. So, please: CREATE.

# 56
# Light it Up

"Why are you depressed?"

I remember my mom asking me this throughout my young life.

I would often just give her a shoulder scrunch implying I didn't know. But what I was probably thinking was, *Well, do you have approximately 97 hours to sit down and listen to all the complex reasons, all the ways the heartache in my life has snowballed into one giant avalanche? Oh wait, I can't do that because I don't even fully understand why nor do I have the mental capacity to even have any conversation whatsoever, let alone one about my feelings.*

Typically (unless it's triggered by a singular traumatic event), there is not one answer to why we are depressed. Why? Because of years of hurt without healing. Because of genetics. Because of "the way I was raised." Because of the way I *wasn't* raised. Because hurting people hurt people. Because of the way our society is built. Because of the weather. Because of the times I had something precious stolen from me, like my body or my heart. Because I have been rejected more times than I can count. Because I've been rejected and it makes me want to hide away forever. Because of the time I rejected someone but they didn't take no for an answer. Because I believe I am both too much and never enough. Because talking about how I feel physically pains me sometimes.

So the pain just grows. Like an infected wound that needs surgery, not just a bandaid. But surgery is terrifying. Surgery means admitting I need a doctor, and it involves cutting something out, and then it means slow and painful recovery. Surgery means my internal wound becomes external and everyone can see it. And I'm already unloveable, so how could I do this to the people around me?

Somewhere along the line, my heartache became so big that I had no room for passion or dreams.

Maybe you've experienced this, too? What has anxiety, depression, smallness, insecurity, or fear stolen from you?

Maybe your energy to be physically active? Maybe even just your energy to smile and laugh? I think laughter is another kind of gold buried in the human heart. If we dug it up more often in ourselves and gave it to each other more frequently, we'd all be a little closer to healing. When I was little, my best friend and I would regularly DIE of laughter—flat on the floor gasping for air and wiping away the tears that were streaming down our cheeks as we hunched over holding our stomachs because our abs were working out harder than they had in months. It was AMAZING. But at some point in my childhood, I stopped having those laughing attacks. And then, years later, I remember that as I began healing from depression, I felt envious as I started noticing people around me laughing. I wanted that. I wanted to erupt in loud and easy laughter without hesitation, but I was always so stuck in my head that I found being unfiltered in my words or my laughter very difficult. So I started praying for easy laughter, for laughing attacks, and, honestly, that's one of the ways I feel closest to others and to God. I believe laughter is a form of worship.

So, challenge time: can you choose just ONE thing that you used to love, one thing that has been stolen from you, and start brainstorming ways to steal it back?

Even if it's just for five minutes, once a week. Let's start there.

What's something you miss doing? Playing guitar? Singing? Writing? Playing basketball? Going on walks? Painting? Drawing? Laughing with friends?

A quick side note though: one of the reasons we so often fail in trying to add new things in to our life is that we don't realize there is always a cost. Every single minute of your day is filled with something that you choose, even if your choice is something like scrolling through social media to "unwind" after a long day or binging on wine and netflix because you're exhausted.

Steal that time back! Steal it back and use it to chase something that genuinely produces joy in your soul.

#Realtalk time: this is how I wrote this book. I realized that way too often when I found a few minutes of margin throughout my day I would use it to check Instagram. I told myself, "Well, I only have two minutes to spare, so I can't REALLY accomplish anything, so I'm just gonna take a break and mindlessly scroll through Instagram." But then I realized what I was doing, and I got *pissed.* I started getting proactive and decided to use those two minutes to write or to think about writing or to read things that would help me with my writing.

I'm not saying this has to be something huge. You don't have to write a book, and you don't have to stop your whole life just to pursue your passion. Start with five minutes a week, that's all. Or start with the two-minute in-between times when you're in the bathroom or waiting in line at the grocery store. Eventually, the fire will grow, you will start allocating more time for chasing your dream, and it will become easier with time. The more you do it, the more you will want to do it.

Go ahead and jot down that one thing here in the margins, or in your notebook, or in your phone, or on a sticky note, or on a receipt. Wherever. Just write it down. But *also* write down the thing you'll be replacing it with, even if it's embarrassing because you don't want to write down "when I'm pooping." Baby steps are king, remember? Jot it down! The thing you want to do is > the thing you want to do less of. And I want you to literally use the greater than sign. And remember, start small: don't write down "songwriting > sunday morning church" or "interior design > showering." Let's just not, okay? Choose a small thing. Examples could be things like:

"Gardening > Fake Pinterest garden planning." You want to garden? As you walk by your garden on your way to the mailbox, pick out ONE singular weed. Or, as you feel tempted to spend the next two hours pinning zen garden designs which you will of course perfectly execute in your entire backyard one day, go repot that one plant that is almost about to die instead.

"Interior Design > Instagram stalking that one girl who is actually designing things." You want to do interior design? Put up ONE frame when you feel tempted to stalk that girl with the perfect minimalist Instagram page. Rearrange one piece of furniture. Get rid of one item thats cluttering your space and making it less lovely and pinterest-y than you'd like.

We have to fuel our lifelessness with the things that once gave us life. It will feel like pulling teeth at first—painful and something you *have* to do but absolutely positively do not WANT to do. It's okay if it feels like a chore at first; I promise the flame will slowly start to grow.

Friends, you *need* to share your voice.

And no, that's doesn't mean you have to stand up in a group and say, "Hi, I'm Betsy, and I'm depressed" (although that's not a bad idea either. I heart Betsy.).

No, I mean *really* share your voice.

Depression has a way of making us believe that our voice isn't important or valuable, that we're better off staying silent and small.

Maybe you're thinking, *What does that look like though? Sharing my voice when most of my days are spent alone or I'm too busy to even hear myself think or, when I finally am with people, I struggle to speak out at all because my brain is so jumbled and I doubt myself?* I get it! I was there for so many days, weeks, years. Some days I *still* have to remind myself to speak up and speak freely. It's awful to be in a room and not know how to be yourself because you don't even know what "being yourself" means anymore.

Here are a few more ideas that have helped me. You don't have to become an overnight extrovert, write a book, give a Ted Talk, or even talk out loud at your book club (but all of that would be awesome too.). Maybe instead, you start a blog. And don't just keep 32 drafts on the digital shelf and let them collect dust either—actually click

"Publish!" Don't worry if your mom is the only one who reads it initially. People will read it.

More importantly though, the words you have buried in your chest will finally leave their cage. You will feel scared and vulnerable, but you'll also feel relieved and lighter.

If you have zero interest in blogging, that's fine! Just find a way to share your voice. Write. Sing. Speak. Send letters. Take pictures. Start a business. Build stuff. Paint pictures. Express yourself in whatever way feels right. Tell the people in your circle what you think about, care about, worry about, dream about. Share anything on your heart. And if you can't think of anything because it feels like depression has hollowed you out, tell someone what *used* to be near to your heart before it started drowning you. If that feels too long ago and you can't remember a time when you weren't underwater, tell them what you used to dream about as a little kid. Dreams live so closely to our voice that they're kind of like roommates, and they're also sharp weapons against depression and shrinking down. Can you remember yours?

When I was little, I use to stand on top of a small, sandy hill in our backyard and give motivational speeches for the trees and the birds (they were a super-attentive audience, by the way). I loved sharing my voice.

But somewhere along the way, people, traumatic events and depression began suppressing me. It makes me cringe to think about how depression subtly shushed me until I believed its lies:

*"Hush. There's no time for you when all of this madness is going on."*

*"Be quiet. Everything you say is stupid."*

*"Just stop. No one wants to listen to what you have to say."*

*"Don't try. Other people's voices and ideas are better than yours."*

Depression whispered into me and shrunk me down until I became convinced my voice had no value. So I stopped using it. For a very long time, I was silent.

You feel me? Does any of that ring true with your soul, too? If so, what do we do? How do we move forward if we can't handle starting a blog or painting a picture? How do we share our voice after such a long season of silence?

Well, we stare the silence down with a little bit of noise. We start creatively sharing our voice, even if it feels awkward or at first sounds like nails on a chalkboard. Start smaller than a blog at first if you need to: maybe start with a text. There were days when all I could do was text because speaking out loud was too much. Start there, even when your fingers weigh a thousand pounds and each and every letter you type is painful. As you lie on your couch for the 4th day in a row, send that text. Tell your friend a story about what you wanted to be when you were little. Tell her what you think is going to happen in the next episode of *This is Us*. Tell her what you wish you had the strength to do or be. Tell him that thing you wanted to say but didn't because you doubted yourself and so the words never came out. Type it slowly. Then send it.

Friend, your voice has value. You don't have to doubt yourself anymore.

Not only does your voice have value, but the rest of us actually need to hear what you have to say.

We need each other to share our voices. Our thoughts and ideas aren't meant to compete with one another, but rather to complete one another.

If depression stole your voice from you, start taking steps to steal it back.

Soon you might start noticing your words are lighter and easier to get out.

And as your words become lighter, you might too.

57
# Safe Place

We showered with the lights off tonight. It wasn't romantic though. I was actually quite lonely. It wasn't an active choice, to shower with the lights off. It just sort of happened. Ricky and I shower almost every night together. Rarely does any you-know-what go down during our nighttime showers (honestly, the shower is too small and it just doesn't work out well for anybody). We do it just to connect, to unwind, to chat about the day as we shampoo, and hop into our bed fresh so that snuggling isn't gross (because no one wants to snuggle with someone's sweat from a long day).

We kept the lights off because, well, we'd been arguing. And you only really notice you're naked after a fight.

Writing a song and showing your husband, which I had just done earlier that evening, feels a lot like sex. You sing the thing, start to finish, and it feels like for three and a half minutes you're Rose on the Titanic posing naked for Jack, hoping he sees at least a little bit of beauty when he looks at you.

However, when the song was finished and I asked him what he thought, he said something along the lines of, "It's nice, but I think you can do better." Now, coming from anyone else, that would have been fine and dandy honest feedback. But that night, I was feeling extra vulnerable and interpreted what he said as, "I see you. And I don't like any of it." That is NOT what he meant, obviously. He's so incredibly supportive of me and my dreams. He just didn't know I was feeling sensitive and how much more his input mattered than most people (I didn't realize either at the time). So I fumbled around and tried to quickly "put my clothes back on," hiding my heart and my hurt.

I tried to tell him that I didn't like his feedback, but I didn't yet have the words (or understanding) to describe what I was *actually* feeling. "Give me something more!" I said. "You can't just say you don't like it. What do you not like about it?" And when he didn't know what to say, I pressed on: "It feels like you just don't care enough to give me good feedback."

But soaping up in the dark, together yet alone, I realized it actually had nothing to do with the not-so-good song that I had written earlier that day and much more to do with *me*. I can hear feedback on pretty much anything, from anyone, and I don't give a rip. In fact, I highly value straightforward constructive criticism. Ricky knows that I don't like sugar-coated feedback which may have been why he wasn't overly concerned about how his input might have made me feel. He was kind and honest with his feedback, nothing wrong with it whatsoever. In fact, coming from anyone else, I probably would've just brushed it off or even felt complimented: "You're right! I can do better! I'm awesome. Thanks for believing in me."

But I'm learning that when it comes to my husband, it's so different. When I share pieces of myself, my dreams, my hopes, my songs, my heart, he isn't just anybody. He's Jack the Painter who's artist eye I value most. And I'm Rose. Naked Rose. And when he can't find something lovely about a song I've written, it *feels* (even if it's untrue) like he can't find something lovely in *me*. And all of a sudden I'm so aware of my skin, exposed and imperfect, and I just want to hide it away in the dark.

Dreams take up so much square footage in our hearts. They are the songs we have yet to write, the paintings we have yet to prop up on our easels, the stories we have yet to tell, the pieces of our soul we have yet to free.

We marry and we hope our dreams—our souls—are safe. And when they're not, we keep the lights off.

But it really doesn't matter if you're married or single. We dream because we long to hear "The gold inside of you is worth sharing." We long to create *because we were created*—creativity is written into our DNA simply because, I believe, we bear the image of God—a God who's favorite pastime is to make beauty. We dream because we can't not dream, and if we find ourselves unable to dream or if we haven't for a long time, there's a good chance that at some point someone we trusted (a teacher, a spouse, a sibling, or, more often than not, a parent) made us feel like those dreams weren't safe to come out. So we keep not turning the light on. We stay in hiding.

My man is so supportive; he cheers me on in my dreams more than almost anyone in my life. But on this one night, he communicated a thing to me in a way that made me disappear inside my turtle shell. He loves me endlessly, but that doesn't mean that *sometimes* he doesn't unintentionally hurt me, just like I sometimes unintentionally hurt him. So many times when a person close to our heart says something to pierce it, it's out of simply not knowing the impact. He had no idea that his feedback on a song I was writing translated as feedback about my actual soul (and, in his defense, neither did I in the moment). If he did, he would have handled his words far more delicately. Other times, a person close to our heart pierces ours out of fear or insecurity, wanting to keep us or themselves safe. They shut us down, and we keep ourselves and our dreams small. There is always a root reason we've been shut down, and it is *never* due to our worthiness. But unfortunately, regardless of the underlying reasons, all we hear in the moment is, "There's nothing in you worth painting."

So we turn lights off.

Well, let me just say this. You *are* worth painting. Every piece of you. You are worth digging up every dream your soul has ever whispered—big or small—and painting it onto a canvas for eyes to see.

The hard part is that our dreams *must* feel safe and unashamed before they are willing to come out. So what do we do when someone or some season in our life has hurt us enough that our light's been shut off for years? Where do we find that safety? Of course, you can reconcile the safety with the relationships in your life. This section was actually born out of a letter I wrote to Ricky to describe how what he said made me feel and why it was about so much more than just a song. Now he knows. He knows that when I show him a song I'm working on, it's pieces of my soul that I'm letting him hold for a few minutes, and he handles them with care. He knows that he is my safe place where I can bring anything to the table (no matter how terrible of a song it is) and he will still tell me, "I think you're so beautiful when you write music." It's not that way with everyone, either. I have a coach who upon hearing an idea or piece of writing I've done has quite literally told me, "Nope. That's bad. Try again." And I love the honesty and get right to work without flinching. But I don't feel naked with him. He's not my safe place. There is a time and place for both types of people in our life.

Showing yourself fully to a *very select* few people whose input we value most can't be because we want their approval but because we allow ourselves to be the most naked with them. These are the people we feel safe to show our earliest drafts to. They are the ones that love us to pieces, no matter how broken our pieces feel.

But what about when the hope of reconciling with those people feels scary? Maybe we're not quite ready to have that hard conversation with our parent, our sibling, our spouse, or whoever. What then? How do we convince our dreams that it's safe to show their faces anyway?

We've got to get serious about sitting in silence with God (if that's how you roll) and making space for those soul-whispered dreams to show up. *We* have to be the safest place for our dreams.

## 58
# How to Make Safe Space So They Show Up

If you're with me when I say God put jewels inside of you, then the obvious first step is to talk to God about your dreams. It can be simple really: "God, would you unearth the jewels in me? Show me how you've created me, what you've specifically molded me for. Give me eyes to see what you see in me."

And then we wait for an answer, and while we wait *we play*.

Have you ever been around a person who made you feel like you weren't allowed to make a mistake? If you spilled water, it was as if you spilled face-melting lava all over the kitchen table. If you missed the winning shot in a game, it was as if a precious gem slipped between your fingers and fell into the ocean. Taking too long to change a tire was like taking too long to deactivate a nuclear bomb. If you said the wrong thing, breathed the wrong way, or walked the wrong way, you were reprimanded, made fun of, or shut down.

Those people are no fun to be around, right?

Well, when our dreams aren't allowed to make a mistake, *we* become the tyrant nitpicking every move, and *we* are the ones who are no fun to be around. No wonder they stay hidden within us. When we aren't willing to play with our dreams, they won't ever want to come out.

So again, how do get them to start showing up? We play.

Say you want to be a painter, but every time you try, you hate what you see on the canvas and pack up all your brushes and stuff them in a drawer. Try painting with your non-dominant hand. Paint with a blindfold on. Set a goal to paint the ugliest picture that has ever been painted. If you give that dream room to breathe without the pressure to perform, over time, jewels will start peeking their heads out and placing themselves on top of that canvas. I promise.

I wanted to be a songwriter more than anything. It's all I did as a child: I wrote stories and songs. I had an entire journal full of them. But somewhere along the way I was convinced I wasn't a songwriter at all.

Twenty-something years later, I went to Nashville with my brother to spend a weekend with some really amazing songwriters. During one of the writing sessions I started silently panicking. I felt so inadequate in a room with so many talented people. Anthony, my brother, immediately sensed I was shutting down. He paused the session and had me get in the vocal booth with headphones on. He started the track and had me sing freestyle with the autotune cranked up all the way on my voice. Basically, aside from sounding like T-Pain, it gave me the freedom to play around without ever singing off pitch. His point, so beautifully illustrated, was that he wanted me to let myself have fun without the pressure to be perfect. He told me about how one of the writers said that the reason she's so incredible is because (and I quote) "she's written 300 crappy songs." *Oooooh.* So she gave herself permission to suck. She spent hours playing. And that is precisely why now she gets paid to do it. She gave her songwriting jewels a chance to breathe.

In a nutshell, I learned that day that if I give my dreams the space to suck, they will be able to breathe again.

I have a very small group of people that I show early drafts of anything I write and whose opinions I actually care about. Otherwise, the songs in my heart (and all of my dreams) know they have space to suck alone with me. I am the safe place for them. I give my dreams the permission to play without the pressure to be perfect, and that's precisely why I will be successful. By the way, I took up that songwriter's advice, and I am now on "crappy song" number 16 out of 300.

## 59
# The In-between

My friend Dean is a crazy-talented musician. He says that when you're writing music you're just playing around with melodies, like trying on different outfits. "Don't overcomplicate it. Just try it on. If you like it, cool. If you don't, put it back." I love the simplicity of that advice. As I write my own music, I don't have to be afraid of singing a new melody for the first time. My identity is not wrapped up in that melody. I haven't "bought" anything yet, so if I decide I don't like the way it fits, I can just put it right back on the hanger. Writing a melody I don't keep doesn't make me a bad songwriter. It makes me a willing one, and it's only the willing ones who write anything worth listening to.

What Dean didn't mention was that as we try on different outfits and when we strip off the ones that don't quite fit right, there's a really awkward in-between time where we're completely naked. We flip through outfits or melodies hoping we'll find a sound or look we like, but at the same time we're growing ever more aware of how exposed we feel.

Those in-between, naked moments can be so scary. They can feel like confusion, questioning, doubting yourself, embarrassment for even trying, insecurities...*all* the "vulnerability hangovers," as Dr. Brené Brown would say. On and on the nakedness goes. But the worst thing we could do is leave on something we can hardly breathe in just because we're a little scared of a few moments of exposure (and no, I do not condone flashing your neighbors; just stick with the metaphor and get your head out of the gutter. Geez!).

When we allow ourselves to be naked as we navigate who we are, what our dreams are, and who we were created to be...*that's* when we bloom. That's when we are really brave, and when we find out that it wasn't really about finally finding the perfectly on-fleek outfit. It was about the *process* of finding it, the process of having the courage to strip off what felt familiar for so many years and sit naked on our bed for a moment to ask ourselves, "What should I wear? What if I have nothing to wear? What if nothing fits right?" While we wrestle with our nakedness, the solution comes to us. God puts together the perfect outfit for us when we allow ourselves to be *seen* on the way to who we want to be. Seen by Him, seen by others, seen by those in whom we've learned to trust along the way. In those naked, in-between outfit moments of vulnerability and exploration lies the true road to becoming a freedom fashionista.

## 60
# Freedom Fashion

More and more, we are moving away from perfect formulas in fashion. You can wear black and brown together now. You can wear denim on denim if you freaking own it, and sneakers are the new stilettos. We are wearing stripes with animal print, graphic tees with fancy blazers. We are valuing second-hand thrift store sustainability over high-end status symbols. We are valuing freedom and expression above fitting in. It's just a matter of whether or not we have eyes to see it and the courage to try it.

I always considered myself to *not* be fashionable at all, but what I realized was that it was less about me not having taste and more about me wanting to stay safe. The question I started asking myself in all areas of my life was this: is this outfit/accessory a safe choice that I'm making out of fear? Am I hesitating to wear the Cuban head wrap, rock the loud orange pants, speak up during meetings, or publish a dang book because it's outside of my comfort zone? Or because I'm worried about what someone might think? Or because I'm nervous I'll mess it up? I was so afraid of standing out that I stayed silent, safe, and small instead. And it was okay for a while until I realized it was suffocating the life out of me entirely. You can't stay small in some areas of your life and assume smallness won't seep into the rest: not letting yourself dream freely doesn't just decrease your ambitions and passions, it destroys your joy and your peace.

Some of us might hesitate with stripping off the smallness narrative because we think it's the righteous thing to do: aren't we supposed to be good, humble people who "make little of ourselves and much of God?" Shouldn't we avoid walking around larger than life and coincidentally walking all over other people? YES. I'm into the heart of those perspectives, but out of context they're just a crutch. I didn't sing during worship at church for the longest time because I "wanted to give other people the chance to shine." At the time, that was genuine. I wanted to be a leader who was more interested in sharing the stage than staying in the spotlight, and I think that's such an important thing to regularly do as a leader. But buried beneath that "altruistic" motive was actually a lot of fear. I had to get really honest with myself. I had to admit that I wanted to sing more than anything. I wanted to sing out loud even if I sang off-key. I had to embrace the fact that not sharing my gifts wasn't doing anyone any favors, and I also had to realize that there's more power in sharing the stage and inviting others to be brave along *with you* than never stepping on it at all.

I shared a vulnerable spoken word poem at church a few weeks ago. A few days before, I had shared it with a small group of friends, and our worship pastor asked me if I'd perform it at the following church service. This immediately gave me the nervous poops, obviously. When Sunday came, I almost didn't get through it. I tried to start speaking but started crying. My voice shook; I had to turn around for a second to recenter, and all along I was really hoping our worship pastor had a plan B in case I croaked all together. But somehow, through all the tears and the trembling, I spoke. And do you know what it did? It not only freed *me*, it helped free others, too. It inspired a number of my friends to write poetry, too. I got messages from so many people telling me they needed to hear those exact words that I had spoken.

What I learned that day was that making little of the gifts God put inside of me isn't humility. It's making little of God.

And I'll tell *you* the same thing.

Staying small or quiet isn't a noble sacrifice. It robs you and the rest of the world from the freedom that comes with sharing the gold inside of you.

This is it, sisters. You've hung in here with me as we've walked through the six main strings—the six main themes in my life—that I had to strip off in order to step into freedom. And now it's your turn. So, what are your strings? What's keeping you small, safe, scared, sad? What's keeping you from fully breathing? What's *too tight*, keeping your gorgeous rib cage from expanding fully?

STRIP IT OFF, GIRL.

Cut those strings no matter how long it takes you, how painful it feels, or how momentarily naked you feel. Stretch out, take a deep breath, and step into your strength, your Girlish Vigor.

**Strip Off: Gunk Covering Your Gold**

The only way to get out of the drought is to let all the insecurities, all the self doubt, out on table and into the light. Let them be seen. Like pieces of dirt hiding jewels for a Queen. Which, *you are* and *I am* royalty. And to think there isn't gold buried in us, weighing us down because it needs to come out, is a lie. It's a lie that you were made to stay silent instead of shine. It's a lie that what you have inside you can't change *his* life, or *her* life, or *mine*. So do us all a favor, and let *all* your pieces see the sun. Where we can see them, and you can run *free*.

**Step Into: Your Girlish Vigor**

The amazing thing about Girlish Vigor is that it can unite us all in such a powerful way while also being incredibly personal. What it means to me will be wildly different from what it means to you, and that's the beauty of it.

**GV Fashion Tip**

What's a Girlish Vigor outfit? Girl, it's YOU. It's you wearing courage. It's you stepping into who you were made to be, unapologetically. Mix your patterns. Put a belt over a few layers. Love what you're wearing even if no one else does. Love who you are even if not many do. Live out your

BIG love for fashion even if you feel tempted to get small and wear something safe. Wear something brave instead.

*Bravery is always in season; wear it boldly.*

# Acknowledgements

There is a tribe of people without which the creation of this book would not have been possible. They are the heartbeat of this project. They have selflessly poured into me with so many hours of encouragement, creativity, logistical planning, support, and prayers.

Words just aren't good enough to thank you all, but I'm going to try anyway.

To the beautiful Girlish Vigor Launch Team—all 200 of you (I mean, what?!)—I am just floored, humbled, and weepy over how you all eagerly got behind this book. I was nervous my launch team would consist of my mom and my husband (a rockin' party of 2), but then *you all showed up* to give this book its wings. I cannot thank you enough. When women (and a few really amazing bros, too) gather in celebration instead of competition, we move mountains together. Thank you. Veronica, Bev, Lib, Liz, Bethany—my magical Hip Hop Girls—thank you for all the laughs, awkward body rolls, and encouragement. You all were such a breath of fresh air during this crazy season. When I talk about dancing freely in this book, I think of our little group every time. And Veronica, your daily MP prayers for me, some days, we're the only thing that kept me writing and persevering. Thank you. I love you ladies. Colleen:

Sister, you are the definition of Queen: you are elegant, charming, confident, and you go out of your way to see your people—your sisters—succeed. That moment when you told me, "Your dreams are my dreams," I knew God had allowed me to cross paths with a once-in-a-lifetime friend. Thank you for being along for this ride every step of the way. With every change of plans, you responded with grace, understanding, and excitement at whatever direction God wanted to take with this thing. Thank you for being such a beautiful friend. Suze: Girl, I don't know if I've ever had a sister so quickly get in my corner to cheer me on, after just spending five minutes with me. You have been through it all, sister. And yet, you turn around and fight for and love your people tirelessly. I don't know if I would have had the courage to do some of these things without your encouragement in those early stages. I love you. Kimberly: thank you for being such a special part of my story. Thank you for being the first counselor to ever really see my soul and not just my diagnosis. You are a rare gem, and I'm so thankful. Love you. Jason, you were the first person to tell me I could do this and then show me the road map. You said, "Let's make a plan," and then, no matter how busy we all got, you never stopped encouraging me or holding me accountable to goals. Thank you, Bro, for being the type of leader that equips others to lead and dream too. Alex: Thank you for being the kind of friend that is willing to brainstorm new book concepts with me every other week and not grow tired of it. Everything you do or are a part of, whether mothering, painting, playing or praying, it's always art and it's always beautiful. You have been such an objective and safe place for me to come to for dreaming, processing and breathing. Thank you, friend. Love you. Amy Simmons: There were some mornings when I was "training" you, that you were actually "training" me. Encouraging me. Championing me. Listening to all my crazy ideas and dreams in-between sets of push-ups. You are a kind, courageous, and patient friend. Thank you for believing in me, and investing in me. I am better because of it. I love you! Mariah B: Thank you for being a sweet friend and the best hair stylist. Every time I come in its like hanging out with my girl and less like an appointment. Thank you for being excited about this project, brainstorming fashion ideas and quotes with me. You're the kind of woman that helps other women stand taller, feel lovely, and believe in themselves. Oh, and I still think we could do our own comedy routine. We are amazing. You're amazing. Love you. Sarita Fouts, you have been such an encouragement and source of joy for me through all of this. Sometimes we have brave friends whose vulnerability in life empowers you to share your own story bravely. You've been that friend to me. Thank you for being a safe place to process, dream, and feel whatever I needed to feel. What you've walked through in life is no small thing, and you use your story to help free the people around you just by living your own story in a raw, real, and beautiful way. Love you hermana. Kaitlin, we've been soul sisters since the moment we met standing in line at She Speaks. I was instantly drawn to your spirit. Thank you for being such a supporter of this project and of me. Even from afar, friendship with you is easy, and chasing dreams alongside you is even easier. Let's always share the stage with each other, girl. Love you. Kenzie, it doesn't matter how much time has passed, when we're together it's like none has passed at all. Friendship with you, even all those years ago, taught me so much about a "girlish vigor" sisterhood, because you are as authentic as it gets. I love you. Justin: Bro! You have been such a dedicated friend to both Ricky and me. Thank you for always checking in about the book. Thank you for being such an encourager. I am waiting for your first finished draft, bro!! Natalia, you me and Ame were the original book-launching Musketeers. The things I learned from you, your confidence, strategies, and spirit-filled approach, gave me the courage and tools to even try! I'm so thankful for the voice you've been in my life and for this book. Love you girl. Johnny, what kind of a bro signs up to help a friend for a last-minute urgent project and then BLOWS IT OUT OF THE WATER? *You do.* You are that friend. You are one of the most talented humans I know and I am just awestruck that you said yes to teaming up on this. Thank you for giving your time so selflessly. I am so grateful, love you Bro. Michelle, the countless hours you have poured into loving me, mentoring me, showing me tools for trauma recovery, and being like a second mom to me, are well, priceless. You are the kind of person who helps others breathe a little more freely in her presence. You are the definition of Girlish Vigor. I love you and am beyond humbled that our paths and families crossed paths and merged. Jackie, girl you have been a cheerleader and supporter of me without hesitation. No matter what ideas I threw at you for this project, you were a "yes" girl. Thank you for your courage, love, and for using your gifts to bless this. I love you! Kati Thompson: you never let me make myself small. You push me to be better, you don't let me get lazy, you love me with my flaws and speak life into who I was made to be. You tell me, "Let the real you out more. Be that girl when you go on stage." And it brings me to tears, because I wish every woman had a Kati in her life. Thank you for supporting this project in so many monumental ways. Thank you for being SUCH a woman of

Girlish Vigor. I love you. Lauren C: Sister, you were one of the first to walk with me during some of the hardest seasons of my life. The woman you are has helped shape the woman I am today, and I can't thank you enough for that. I can't thank you enough for your love, compassion, and wisdom that you have just poured on me over the years. I love you so much sister. Martha: oh, Sister. Thank you. For so many things. Too many to put here. Thank you for spending hours of your precious time away from your own projects and on mine instead. Thank you for staying up late to edit and be the best writing consultant. Thank you for caring about this book as if it were your very own baby. Thank you for being the one to ask me, "Are you afraid no one will want to support you?" when I told you I was considering not launching the book with an official team. Thank you for being such a light in my life during such a hard season. You've been such a friend to me. Lauren M: it was always my dream to have a sister, and God gave me you. Thank you for being there through every season, and now this one. As we mother, teach, and pursue dreams alongside one another, I think of our nights spent watching the same two movies on repeat (The Wedding Planner and Mary Kate and Ashley, of course.) It was those sweet moments just hanging out in pajamas, laughing, crying, bickering, and whispering that bonded us stronger than any sister genes ever could. Thank you for being gracious, wise, and loving throughout this book launch. Thank you for being my sister. I love you so much. Felicia: Mamacita, Uelita, Super-Grandma. There are so many beautiful roles you've played in my life and my family's life and I cannot thank you enough. How many chapters did I write *only* because you made yourself available to help? How many posts did you share of mine calling me your "beautiful and talented daughter-in-law" that brought a tear to my eye? Thank you for your love, your support, and all of your help. You helped give this book its wings and I could never thank you enough. I love you. Christy: Girl, how many cover drafts did you give me feedback on? Basically a million. And you never grew tired of it. Your selfless support of me has always meant so much. You were one of the first to know I was writing a book when I accidentally left the manuscript out on the kitchen island—and even though I wanted to hide it, you excitedly held it and offered to help edit or do whatever I needed. I've never forgotten that moment. Thank you, sister. Ben and Cassy: first of all, Bro!! Dude, we grew UP together, and now look at us. Chasing dreams and loving on sweet little BG. Cass, you have been such a dear, dear friend to me for so many years now. We've birthed so much life alongside one another (babies, dreams, design companies, books!). You are such a life-giver. Even when you don't realize it. Your words lift my soul in the moments I need it most. And you BOTH have gotten behind this project and supported, sponsored, and even fed us through it. Love you both. Danielle, my sweet Dee! What can I even say? How do you wrap up twenty-something years of friendship and all the ways I could thank you? You have championed me literally through thick and thin, mud and water (and some poop too, obviously). Thank you for offering your art, love, and encouragement so selflessly for every one of my crazy ideas. You are the sister a girl always dreams of having. Oh, and the fact that within just about the same month you will have birthed your first baby and I will have birthed my first "book baby"? It's just too much—the way God always aligns our paths in the most creative ways. I love you. I love just being along for the ride with you, life is so much richer because of you. Steve: in so many moments of my life you were the counselor and friend who helped me find healing truth. You are one of my greatest teachers. If there is ever a person that finds freedom from my words, that is freedom and healing *you* likely sprung into life first. Thank you for being the kind of teacher whose fingerprints will land on the healing stories of so many souls. Rob and Amy. Team Seiffert, what in the actual world did I ever do to deserve you? I did nothing.

Not a single thing, and that's the whole thing. That's the reason I get weepy just thinking about it. You two just love me sacrificially, taking precious time away from your families to help this dream fly. I had no idea what I was doing and you two led the way. You treat me like we are blood and it overwhelms me with gratitude. I'm humbled. Seriously. If it wasn't for you two I would have basically just written this book on a napkin and offered it at a lemonade stand for 50 cents a pop. But you guys have used your gifts to make it magic. Thank you for being my family. Rob, you're my brother and designer and it's a gift I don't deserve. Ame, you're my artist, coach, and soul sister in so many ways. You're the one that blazed the trail in front of me. I feel humbled and privileged to get to chase dreams next you, Sister. Thank you both for your grace and overly-generous love. I love you both so much. Sarah: my girl. My soul sister. If there is a friend who's seen my ugliest, most raw pieces and never flinched once, never hesitated to embrace me all the more after seeing it all, Girl, it was you. You are the kind of gem that only comes around once a lifetime. Thank you for the time you spent looking at this work, giving feedback and brainstorming with me. Thank you for being such a healing presence in my life—the kind of friend that literally draws out the Girlish Vigor in me when I can't seem to find it. Thank you for loving not only me, but my entire family so well. I love you, Sister. Ben and Leslie, you two have been in my corner since day one. You have loved us, coached us, supported us. Ben, you push me to be better and it's the kind of brotherhood most sisters just wish for. Leslie, all you have to do is get on Marco Polo and I am convinced that everything is going to be okay. You're the kind of woman that other women feel safe to stand taller around, because you draw out the best in us. You find the person in the room who needs love and you love the crap out of them. I love you, Sister. Thank you both for your endless support and encouragement for this project. Lana. Mi Lanitas! Hermanita, from the moment I met you I knew you were my sister. Laughing comes easily around you. Breathing comes easily around you. Friendship comes easily with you. You're the kind of beauty that invites others to breathe freely, and that's Girlish Vigor right there. Not to mention, you are the OG of Girlish Vigor. You were the one willing to get in my corner and believe in this dream before anyone else even knew it existed. It takes such a strong woman to lift up the women around her, and you do it effortlessly. I love you and am so, so grateful for you. Libby. Ohhhhh, Libsta. You have been my sidekick, my sanity, and mostly, my sister. You know my schedule better than I do, and some days, you even know my heart better than I do. Girl. When I say this book and launch would not have happened without you, I don't mean that metaphorically. I mean literally, you are the one that gave this little engine its fuel. You are the one that fought for the necessary details when I just couldn't even. Thank you, from the bottom of my growing little vigorous heart. Thank you. I love you. Also, Girl, you're next. Get ready. Alina, you're always down. Down to write songs with me, down to edit books with me, down to sit and dream about the beach with me. Down to share our hearts—the ugly and the beautiful. Down to dance with me and have wine (or whiskey) while we write music and chase dreams. I can't believe I get to call you both friend and sister. Thank you for all the time you poured into this project—literally hours upon hours upon hours. It would not be the same without you. I love you, Hermana. Duran clan: I am the luckiest girl in the entire world because I married into this incredible tribe. Thank you for welcoming me with open arms, lots of food, and that Latin love I missed from not being around my family. Thank you for supporting me, as if I were your blood. I love you all so much! García clan: mi familia bella. What did I ever do to deserve being a part of this incredible family? The way we love each other is something rare. The way we dance, laugh, and have each others' backs is just incredible. We challenge each other to be better. To reach for the stars. I'm so grateful. Los quiero tanto. Abby y Abuelo - ¿Qué les puedo decir? Ustedes son la razón que estamos aquí hoy en este paiz de libertad. Libertad—el tema central y más significante de éste libro—lo empecé aprendiendo de ustedes primero. Gracias por todos los sacrificios, y por trabajar tan duro por nuestra familia. Ustedes y mis Abuelos De La Torre son los que lo empezaron todo. Ustedes son la razón por la cual puedo hoy yo, una niña de raíces cubanas... escribir palabras en una página sin miedo a nada. Los quiero tanto. Anthony: my baby bro. You are so much more of a big brother than a baby brother to me at this point in our lives, aren't you? How many times have you called me and known just what to say to encourage me? How many times have you gone out of your way to facetime me just to spend time together even though you were across the country? From our gut microbiomes to our hearts, we are siblings. Twins, even. You believe in me in moments when I YELL at you and say "I'M DONE." You don't let me quit. You fight for me. You push me to better. You love me selflessly. I'm so proud of you. I'm so grateful for you. Thank you for all of the time you spent on this project with me; brainstorming, dreaming, planning, editing photos. None of this would be what it is without you. I love you. Dad, I wanted to get my PhD just because you have it. I've always said I was your mini-me. And now that I've finished a book, I believe it more than ever. Because people like us take all the hard things that happen in life and make them into something positive. You've always been such a powerful and positive force in my life. Thank you for believing in me. Thank you for all the ways that you love and support us. I love you, Daddy. Mimi: thank you for entering our family and loving, encouraging, and supporting us fiercely. We love you. Nick: my incredible big brother. If there was a heavy lifter to this project Arnold Schwarzenegger-style, it would be you. The mountain of tasks you've handled for this is sky-high. And you never once ask for anything in return. You just keep loving me. Believing in me. Selflessly giving of your time (literally into the wee hours of the night.) You tell me my dreams are too small and that I'm capable of so much more. I love you so much, Bro. I'm so thankful. Mom, Mama, my sweet Mamacita. You were the one who kept all my stories, journals, drawings, and songs recorded on that old tape recorder. You were the first one to believe in me. You were the one that told me, "Gelly, is personal training what you love? You love music. You love art. You love writing." And you were right, Mama. You're right so often and it just takes me time to realize it for myself. Thank you for being such a woman of Girlish Vigor. You taught me by example to chase my dreams (even if it meant middle-of-the-night-studying), fight for freedom for others, welcome all into my home, and be true to myself. Thank you for all of the time and energy you have put into this book. Thank you for your humility as I talked about hard things. I love you, Mama. I would not be half the woman I am today if it wasn't for you. Meli: my baby girl. You won't read this for a few years, but when you do, I want you to know you are the reason Mommy started writing again. It was as I held you at 1 and 2 (and 4) A.M. that I started stitching these words together as I nursed and held you. Your sweet face: you are the reason Mommy is who she is today. And I hope seeing me be brave and write this book teaches you that you can do *anything*! Ricky: my Ricky. Babe, I paused on that period after your name for a while. Like, awkwardly long. Because I wish you could just "feel ma hart" instead of read these words—I got to your name and this heart of mine started racing. I can't possibly find words to thank you. YOU of all people have loved me and this book more than anyone else. You have spent time wrestling with these words to make them the best they could be (and with not a whole lot of time at your hands). You took my mangled first draft and turned it into a book. YOU were the originator of Girlish Vigor (surprise, everyone reading this! Ricky invented GV. What a guy.) You fight for the women in your life to have a voice even when no one else is willing to. You fought for me even when I couldn't bare to fight for myself. You are the greatest kind of warrior—a warrior for redeemed souls and for freed hearts. Mine beats for you. I love you.

# Notes

Threads 1-6: Amy Seiffert, all *Girlish Vigor illustrations*, www.amyseiffert.com, @amyseiffert

Thread 1, Chapter 8: A Final Confession

Hillary McBride, www.hillarylmcbride.com, https://www.instagram.com/p/BvA-QX9phnNs/?utm_source=ig_share_sheet&igshid=1q4ugtbt43rmo. Pg 39

Thread 2, Chapter 13: My Body is a Friggn' Wonderland. There. I Said It, and I'm Not Sorry

Hillary McBride, Study "Mother's Daughters and Body Image.", Pg 70, https://itunes.apple.com/us/podcast/for-the-love-with-jen-hatmaker-podcast/id1258388821?mt=2&i=1000427233483

Thread 3: Chapter 19: Stuck on Loop

Dr. Gabor mate, quote from www.drgabormate.com

Thread 4: Chapter 26: Sweatpants and Manicures pg 133

Andrew Solomon, *The Noonday Demon*, (New York, NY: Scribner, 2011) 36-38.

Thread 4: Chapter 34: Girl, Let me Love you— pg 170

John Piper, *When the Darkness Will Not Lift,* (Wheaton, Illinois: Good News Publishers, 2006)

Thread 5: Chapter 37: What Even IS Addiction?

Dr Gabor Mate, quote from www.drgabormate.com, 182

Thread 5: Chapter 43: Little Pills and Mountain Tops

Johann Hari, *Lost Connections,* (Buffalo, NY: Bloomsbury USA, 2018) Excerpt from Joe Rogan Podcast.

Andrew Solomon, *The Noonday Demon*, (New York, NY: Scribner, 2011) 21

Thread 5: Chapter 48: "The way things should be" pg 240

Amanda Cook, Song quote: *Pieces*